Chocolate Days

Achingly Delicious Recipes When Only Chocolate Will Do

Laurie Watts

PRIMA PUBLISHING

PRIMA PUBLISHING and its colophon, which consists of the letter P over PRIMA, are trademarks of Prima Communications, Inc.

Library of Congress Cataloging-in-Publication Data

Watts, Laurie
  Chocolate days : achingly delicious recipes when only chocolate will do / Laurie Watts.
    p.   cm.
  Includes index.
  ISBN 0-7615-0116-9
  1. Cookery (Chocolate)   I. Title.
  TX767.C5W38 1995
  641.6'374—dc20   95-21227
                                                 CIP

96 97 98 99 AA 10 9 8 7 6 5 4 3 2 1

Printed in the United States of America

How to Order

Single copies may be ordered from Prima Publishing, P.O. Box 1260, Rocklin, CA 95677; telephone (916) 632-4400. Quantity discounts are also available. On your letterhead, include information concerning the intended use of the books and the number of books you wish to purchase.

To Dale,

who fills my Chocolate Days with love and laughter,

and my Chocolate Nights with . . . inspiration!

Contents

When Only Chocolate Will Do . . .   x
*We asked friends to confide their favorite chocolate indulgences,
and then fantasized about how to make their treats
richer, sweeter, lighter, or even more chocolatey!*

Tips for Chocolate Bliss   xi
Keep a few simple tips in mind and you can master any chocolate recipe!

The Chocolate Family   xv
Get to know your chocolate choices!

One More Essential Ingredient   xviii
A secret way to enhance your Chocolate Days!

Immediate Gratification Days   1
Quick fixes that combine and "chocolate-up" your over-the-counter favorites!
Cherries Oreo!   3
Quick Café Mocha   4
Banana Bliss   5
Peanut Butter Fudge Bombe   6

Candy Bar Mousse   7

Strawberry S'mores   8

Twinkies Charlotte   9

Mystic Mint Chiller   10

Mari's Brownie Binge   11

Fill Your Kitchen with Comfort Days   12

Classics from Grandma's warm, loving kitchen!

Toll House Chunks   14

Hot Fudge Pudding Cake   16

Double Chocolate Brownies   18

Buttercream Layer Cake   20

Chocolate Apple Streusel   22

Starry Night Muffins   24

Chocolate Pound Cake   26

Chunky Junkie Bundt   28

Cocoa Butter Cookies   30

Guilt-Free Days   31

Fabulous, flavorful, reduced-fat pick-me-ups!

Mocha L'Orange Slush   33

Angel Berry Trifle   34

Banana Fudge Muffins   36

IcedWiches   38
Irish Cream Cheese Cups   40
CocoLocos   42
CappCakes   44
Chocolate Ecstasy!   46
Chocolate Mint Clouds   48

Sticky-Sweet Days   49

Fun, white and milk chocolate, extra-sweet treats!
Rainbow Crispies   51
Liar's Dice   52
Banana Split Trifle   54
Macadamia Macaroons   56
Chocolate Pizza   58
Lemon Cream Dreams   60
Tri-Chocolate Pie   62
Peanut Butter Cup Cakes   64
Peaches and Cream Truffles   66

Ultrarich Days   68

Slightly more sophisticated, dark chocolate desserts!
Raspberry Crowns   70
Bittersweet Crème Brûlée   72

French Truffles   74

Biscotti Parfait   75

Bavarian Torte   76

Truffle Tea Cookies   78

Chocolate Truffle Cake   80

Mocha Nirvana   82

Cinnamon Swirl Bread Pudding   84

Chocolate Nights   85

Romantic, sensual dalliances, meant to be shared!

Amourette Cacao   87

Tuxedo Strawberries   90

Pâte Grand Marnier   92

Coupe Glacée Café   94

Crème Praline   96

Fondue Chambord   97

Eggnog Bombe   98

Tiramisu Chocolat   100

Fire & Ice . . . Finger Paints D'Amour!   102

Resources   103

Index   105

Conversion Chart   110

My Heartfelt Thanks

To all the talented, consummate professionals at Prima Publishing, especially my editors Jennifer Sander, for bringing me a brilliant title, and Andi Reese Brady, for helping me turn my raw ramblings into delicious prose. And to Lindy Dunlavey and Kent Lacin for creating an irresistible cover. To Rick and Joyce, who, with the patience of saints, helped me get computer compatible. To Sue, for holding on to our old family recipes. To my "beta taste sites," for selflessly throwing themselves into critiquing my successes and well-intentioned disasters. To Ray and June, for raising me with an appreciation for chocolate and a philosophy that imagination is as important as knowledge. To Nina, for raising my partner with a vision of all that can be and the courage to go after his dreams. To Sam, my sunshine, for showing me the world through new eyes. To Mari, lifelong friend and culinary genius, for always making time to help me brainstorm, troubleshoot, celebrate, and commiserate. To Paula, whose insight, friendship, and scripts help me through even my darkest Chocolate Days, for helping me marry my passion for chocolate with my love for writing. And to Dale, for helping me turn my quest for the ultimate chocolate indulgence into a highly coveted livelihood.

Your belief in me brings out the best in me.

When Only Chocolate Will Do . . .

What's your favorite indulgence when you're having a Chocolate Day? Are you a purist; wanting little more added to your chocolate than more chocolate? Have you joined the new mocha madness; enriching your chocolate with espresso and coffee liqueurs? Or are you a chocolate adventurer; blending rich chocolate with everything from Irish Cream to fruits and nuts?

We asked friends to confide their favorite chocolate indulgences, and then fantasized about how to make those treats richer, sweeter, lighter, or even more chocolatey!

The results? *Achingly delicious* recipes that will transport you to chocolate nirvana!

Special note: For the best ride, use the best chocolate. We prefer Callebaut and Guittard for flavor and consistency, but there are many fine domestic and imported chocolates. Have a "chocolate tasting" and use the pure chocolate you fall in love with in all your favorite chocolate recipes.

Tips for Chocolate Bliss

Your time is valuable, even if you're only taking a few minutes to toss together an "Immediate Gratification" selection. And, if you're having a temperamental Chocolate Day, the last thing you need is for your pick-me-up to taste worse than your mood. So keep a few simple tips in mind and you can master any chocolate recipe!

Start with the Best Ingredients.

Treat yourself to high quality chocolate. In addition to the unparalleled flavor rewards, you'll be amazed at how much easier it is to work with. Choose fresh, whole dairy products (except for some of our reduced-fat recipes) and, whenever possible, natural flavorings. The end result will be more than worth the relatively minimal additional cost.

Invest in High Quality Tools.

Scout your area for specialty pastryware shops or write for catalogs (see "Resources," page 103). Chances are, you'll need only a few tools to create your favorite chocolate treats and spending a little more, for far superior products, will increase your odds for culinary success and save you money in the long run. (Good products last a lifetime.)

Choose Your Storage Conditions Carefully.

Most of us have been spoiled by mass-merchandised candy bars that can travel around in our car for weeks and still taste like they just came off the store shelf. High quality chocolate is dramatically different and should be handled with respect. For optimum flavor, keep it cool (60–65 degrees), dry, and airtight. Refrigerating or storing pure chocolate above 65 degrees may cause the cocoa butter to rise to the top creating grayish streaks or a frosty appearance. Gently melting, blending, and re-tempering (see opposite page) should bring back its gloss and snap, but its flavor may remain slightly diminished. You should be able to store dark chocolate, under the right conditions, almost indefinitely. Milk and white chocolate have a more limited shelf life due to dairy additives. To be safe, check with the manufacturer.

Never Melt Chocolate Over Direct Heat.

Chocolate burns easily! No matter what you've read or been told, play it safe, *never* melt chocolate over direct heat. If you don't own or want to invest in a double boiler, find a bowl in your cupboard that will sit within, yet atop, one of your pots, allowing an inch or two of airspace above the hot (not boiling or even simmering) water in the pot. Break or chop your chocolate into small pieces before placing it in the bowl or double boiler insert and stir often (gently and slowly) with a wooden spoon or high quality rubber spatula. (Don't leave your utensil in warming or hot chocolate!)

Avoid Microwaving Chocolate.

Chocolate burns even faster in the microwave! If you have no other alternative (or if you're whipping up an "Immediate Gratification" quickie) use a medium setting for very short lengths of time and stir the chocolate thoroughly between each interval. Never, *ever*, microwave chocolate on high.

Tempering Chocolate.

You'll want to temper the chocolate you plan to use for dipping fruit or truffles. Also, if your chocolate has been stored in a place that was too warm or too cool, it may have "bloomed," the term used when the cocoa butter has risen to the surface creating grayish streaks or a frosty appearance. To bring the cocoa butter back in balance you must "temper" the chocolate. There are two methods: the traditional method, which has you heat the chocolate to a certain temperature, pour it on a marble slab to cool to another specific temperature, and then reheat it to yet a third temperature; and an easier, shortcut method that keeps the chocolate in the pot and your cleanup to a minimum.

For quick and easy tempering: Chop one pound of chocolate and place 75 percent of it in the top of a double boiler over hot (not boiling) water. Heat dark chocolate to *no higher than* 115 degrees, milk chocolate to *no higher than* 112 degrees or white chocolate to *no higher than* 110 degrees. (Be careful! Remove your chocolate from the heat source before it hits these temperatures as it will continue to escalate even after it's removed.) Add the remaining 25 percent of the chopped chocolate and stir gently and slowly until it's completely melted. Your chocolate should be tempered!

Please note that different manufacturers recommend slightly different tempering temperatures; the temperatures given above are "rule of thumb."

To Make Grated Chocolate, Shavings, or Chocolate Curls:

For grated chocolate or very small shavings, draw a block of chocolate, which has been stored at 60–65 degrees, across your handheld grater. The various grates will determine the types and size of the shreds.

For chocolate shavings, draw your vegetable peeler across a block of chocolate, which has been stored at 60–65 degrees.

For chocolate curls, allow the block of chocolate to warm slightly, then scrape with your vegetable peeler.

To Toast and Grind Nuts:

Toasting brings out the flavor in nuts. To toast, preheat your oven to 350 degrees. Spread the nuts on a jelly-roll or pizza pan. Bake 10–15 minutes, until golden, checking and stirring every five minutes. For hazelnuts, allow them to cool for 10 minutes, then place them in a thin towel and rub them together to remove their skins.

To grind nuts, place them in your food processor, blender, or nut grinder and pulsate until they're ground to a mealy powder. Do not overgrind or they will become oily.

The Chocolate Family

Fine chocolate, like fine wine, is available in many imported and domestic varieties. As burgundy differs dramatically from chardonnay in color, flavor, and body, bittersweet and white chocolate are worlds apart in taste and texture. And, as each vintner has its own formula for selecting and processing grapes, each "chocolaterie" has its own method for selecting, roasting, blending, grinding, and conching (a method of stirring) their precious cocoa beans. The result is a myriad of choices for you; each with its own nuance. Try venturing from the chocolate to which you've become accustomed. You may find one you like even more!

Cocoa Powder

This fine powder is the result of the cocoa butter being removed from chocolate. There are two types of cocoa powder: (1) Pure (non-alkalized) cocoa, which works better when baking; and (2) "Dutch-processed" (alkalized) cocoa, which has a mellower flavor for coating truffles and decorating desserts.

Unsweetened Chocolate

This is chocolate in its purest form; chocolate solids, known as chocolate liquor, and cocoa butter, with only a small addition of vanilla.

Bittersweet Chocolate

A minimal amount of sugar, vanilla, and lecithin are added to the unsweetened chocolate base to provide a very sophisticated flavor.

Semisweet Chocolate

Slightly more sugar is added to the components of bittersweet chocolate to deliver a rich, European favorite.

Sweet or German Chocolate

Slightly more sugar is added to the semisweet version to create this sweetest form of dark chocolate.

Milk Chocolate

Not only more sugar, but powdered milk is added to sweet, dark chocolate to create America's number one choice of chocolate.

White Chocolate

The dark chocolate liquor is removed and sugar, powdered milk, vanilla, and lecithin are added to the base of cocoa butter to offer an ultra-sweet "chocolate" that's rapidly growing in popularity.

Coverture

This term is used for chocolate with the highest ratio of cocoa butter; which usually means the richest flavor.

"Coating" Chocolate

To make it faster and easier for home chocolatiers to prepare chocolate for dipping and molding, some manufacturers offer a chocolate which has had its temperamental, if flavorful, cocoa butter removed and replaced with vegetable oils. Theoretically, this form of chocolate need not be tempered.

One More Essential Ingredient

There's one more essential ingredient to creating achingly delicious chocolate recipes: your style. Don't hesitate to add or substitute flavors and don't underestimate the power of your setting and serving choices. Limoges plates, a crackling fire, and raspy, French cabaret music will help ignite more than your taste buds, enhancing your Tiramisu Chocolat. While nothing makes Toll House Chunks taste quite as good as that funky, pottery plate you found in Laguna Beach, your favorite sweats, and a copy of *Steel Magnolias*. So the next time you're in the mood . . .

Take Yourself Shopping!

Find dessert plates, saucers, and goblets which reflect your chocolate moods. Now, tuck them away for you to use when you're having a Chocolate Day. And when you run across a dish that's deliciously romantic, buy two!

Then, When You Start to Ache . . .

Get comfortable! Slide into your favorite denims or silky camisole. Put on your favorite CD or a tape of that movie you love, light a few candles, take the phone off the hook, break out the chocolate, and unleash your imagination!

Immediate Gratification Days

Some days, you need chocolate and you need chocolate *Now!* You don't have time to bake, nor are you in the mood to fuss. Must you settle for a plain candy bar or simple pre-packaged cookie? Not anymore! Here's how you can, in just a few minutes, turn that candy bar into a heavenly mousse and that cookie into a decadent bite-sized bombe!

And as a bonus, some of these craving-quenchers you can even whip up at the office!

Special Note: We've recommended the national brands which we feel bring you the most achingly delicious results for each treat. If there is another brand you prefer, please feel free to substitute.

Cherries Oreo!

It wasn't easy trying to improve on everyone's favorite packaged cookie, but this little treasure has become the jewel in our crown of chocolate quickies!

1	teaspoon maraschino cherry juice	4	maraschino cherries
1	Oreo chocolate, cream-filled cookie	¼	crumbled Oreo cookie
2	tablespoons Guittard white chocolate chips		

1. Drizzle the cherry juice in a zigzag pattern across your favorite dessert plate. Place the whole cookie in the center of the plate.
2. Microwave the white chocolate, in a heatproof bowl, on MEDIUM power, for ten seconds. Stir gently. Repeat, heating for ten seconds at a time, until the chocolate is mostly melted but still slightly lumpy. Spoon 1½ tablespoons over the cookie.
3. Quickly, remove the stems from 3 cherries and place them, top side down, on the white chocolate-covered cookie. Spoon the remaining chocolate in the center and place the remaining cherry on top. Sprinkle with the crumbled cookie.

Makes one super-sweet treat.

Quick Café Mocha

For me, everyday is a Chocolate Day! This treat starts my day and, sometimes, gives my afternoon a boost. The secret to this espresso-substitute is delicious, fresh brewed coffee and ultrarich ice cream! (If you're adventurous, Häagen-Dazs makes an Irish Cream ice cream.)

1	teaspoon (heaping) Suisse Mocha flavored, instant coffee	1	teaspoon (heaping) Häagen-Dazs* vanilla ice cream
7	ounces hot, freshly brewed coffee	¼	teaspoon sweetened, powdered chocolate

1. Place the instant coffee in a clear-glass, Irish coffee mug.
2. Fill with hot coffee and stir.
3. Microwave on HIGH for 30 seconds.
4. Top with the ice cream and powdered chocolate.

Makes one steamy, creamy mugful.

Banana Bliss

By substituting pound cake for genoise, pudding for pastry cream, bananas for raspberries, and chocolate chips for a chocolate cup, we've come up with a quick version of an elegant French favorite. The only thing missing is sprinkling the cake with liqueur, which would give you an even richer dessert!

1	slice (1 inch) Sara Lee Fresh Baked Butter Pound Cake	½	cup sliced banana
1	Jello chocolate pudding cup (4 ounces)	2	tablespoons Nestle's chocolate chips

1. Place the pound cake on your favorite dessert plate.
2. Spread the chocolate pudding on top.
3. Cover the pudding with the banana slices.
4. Top with the chocolate chips.

Makes one elegant quickie!

Peanut Butter Fudge Bombe

This treat is even more fun to make than it is to eat! If you're in the mood for an even sweeter treat, coat the ice cream with Reese's Pieces before you decorate it with the whipped cream!

1	Pepperidge Farm Chewy Brownie Walnut cookie	1	scoop Ben & Jerry's Peanut Butter Cup ice cream
2	tablespoons Reese's creamy peanut butter	1	can Reddi-wip instant real whipped heavy cream
1	tablespoon Smucker's chocolate fudge topping		

1. Place the cookie on your favorite dessert plate and slather it with peanut butter.
2. Make an indentation, with the back of a teaspoon, in the center of the peanut butter. Pool the fudge topping in the indentation.
3. Place the scoop of ice cream on top.
4. Decorate, covering the bombe entirely, with the whipped cream.

Makes one mini-bombe.

Candy Bar Mousse

Sliding a spoon of this creamy cloud of chocolate into your mouth is like sliding into a silky bubblebath. So close your eyes and enjoy!

3 ounces Guittard milk chocolate, chopped into small pieces	1 candy bar, chopped into bite-sized pieces
¼ cup heavy cream, chilled	

1. Microwave the chocolate, in a heatproof bowl, on MEDIUM power, for 15 seconds. Stir gently and thoroughly. Repeat, heating for 15 seconds at a time, until completely melted and smooth. Set aside to cool to tepid.
2. Whip the cream, with an electric mixer on high, until peaks are firm.
3. Turn the mixer to low and slowly pour the chocolate into the cream until just barely blended. *Don't overmix!* It's okay if the chocolate and cream are not completely integrated. Overmixing will create a sandy texture and you'll be blending the mousse a bit more when you add the candy bar.
4. By hand, with a rubber spatula, gently fold the candy bar into the mousse. Again, *don't overmix!* Spoon into a glorious goblet!

Makes one creamy treat.

Strawberry S'mores

If your idea of camping out is staying at Yosemite's Ahwanee Hotel, here's how you can enjoy this childhood favorite in the backwoods of your own kitchen!

2   Honey Maid chocolate grahams

2   Hershey's milk chocolate candy bars (1.55 ounces each)

2   Kraft large marshmallows, quartered

1   tablespoon Dickinson's strawberry preserves

1. Preheat your toaster oven to 350 degrees and line its tray with foil.
2. Place one chocolate graham on the tray. Top with one chocolate bar.
3. Arrange the quartered marshmallows on the chocolate bar and dab the strawberry preserves on the marshmallows.
4. Top with the other chocolate bar and chocolate graham.
5. Bake for five minutes or until the S'mores begin to ooze.

Makes one sizable oozer!

Twinkies Charlotte

This petite pastry was inspired by its ladyfinger cousin in the French Quarter of New Orleans. Rich chocolate mingles with sweet caramel and buttery pecans to create a chocolate-praline crown for this Twinkie lover's treat!

3	tablespoons Smucker's chocolate sundae syrup	1	large scoop Häagen-Dazs Vanilla Fudge ice cream
3	tablespoons Smucker's caramel sundae syrup	2	Hostess Twinkies
		2	tablespoons chopped pecans

1. Swirl one tablespoon *each*, of the chocolate and caramel syrups, in a lacy pattern on your favorite dessert plate. Place the ice cream in the center.
2. Slice the Twinkies in half, lengthwise. Save the bottoms for another day. Cut the tops in half, widthwise. Place, cut sides down and in, around the scoop of ice cream.
3. Pool the remaining 2 tablespoons *each* of the chocolate and caramel syrups atop the ice cream and crown with pecans.

Makes one petite charlotte.

Mystic Mint Chiller

On Chocolate Days when it's hot and humid outside, try this icy treat. It will cool your body as it soothes your mind!

2   Mystic Mint cookies, quartered
     Several spoonfuls Breyers mint
     chocolate chip ice cream
1   cup ice cold milk

1. Place quartered cookies in the bottom of your favorite dessert goblet.
2. Layer, loosely, with the chocolate mint ice cream.
3. Top with the milk and slide your spoon through the ice cream several times, to slush it up a bit.

Makes one chocolate chiller!

Mari's Brownie Binge

Layers and layers of chocolate! This is a perfect treat for those Chocolate Days when the purist in you doesn't want any other flavor getting in the way of your favorite!

¼ cup heavy cream, chilled
1 teaspoon cocoa powder
1 tablespoon sugar
6 tablespoons Smuckers hot fudge sauce

1 square (2 inches) Sara Lee Fresh Baked Fudge Nut Brownie
1 scoop Ben & Jerry's Chocolate Fudge Brownie ice cream
¼ teaspoon chocolate sprinkles

1. Whip the cream, with an electric mixer on its highest setting, until soft peaks begin to form. Sprinkle in the cocoa powder and sugar while continuing to whip. Refrigerate when thoroughly blended.
2. Heat the fudge topping, according to the directions on the package. Puddle two tablespoons in the bottom of your favorite dessert goblet.
3. Add the brownie and two more tablespoons of hot fudge.
4. Top with the ice cream, the remaining 2 tablespoons hot fudge, the chocolate whipped cream, and the chocolate sprinkles.

Makes one ultrarich binge!

Fill Your Kitchen with Comfort Days

For those days when you need to take a giant step back in time to Grandma's kitchen, where the aroma of whatever was baking greeted you with a warm hug and a promise of good tastes to come, we've gathered recipes for the classics and "chocolated" them up! You'll swoon over our Hot Fudge Pudding Cake and Toll House Chunks, even before they come out of the oven!

Toll House Chunks

One legend tells us this all-time favorite was born when there wasn't enough time to melt the chocolate for the creator's fudge cookies. Another claims she was out of nuts when making her favorite butter cookies. In both legends, the original recipe contained large chunks of chocolate!

1	cup pecans, chopped
1¼	cups flour
½	teaspoon baking soda
½	teaspoon salt
½	cup unsalted butter, softened
½	cup firmly packed light brown sugar
⅓	cup granulated sugar
1	large egg, warmed to room temperature
½	teaspoon vanilla
1	teaspoon praline liqueur
8	ounces milk chocolate, chopped into bite-sized chunks

1. Preheat your oven to 350 degrees. Lightly butter and flour cookie sheets or cover them with parchment paper.
2. Toast the pecans (see "Tips," page xiv); set aside.
3. Sift together the flour, baking soda, and salt; set aside.
4. Cream the butter and sugars, with a mixer on high, until fluffy. Adjust your mixer to medium and add the egg, vanilla, and praline liqueur, one ingredient at a time.
5. By hand, using a rubber spatula, fold in the flour mixture, $\frac{1}{4}$ cup at a time, until the dry ingredients are moistened. *Don't overmix!* Fold in the chocolate and pecans.
6. Drop, by generous teaspoonfuls, onto prepared cookie sheets. Bake 8–12 minutes, until golden brown.

Makes about 40 bite-sized cookies.

Hot Fudge Pudding Cake

One bite of this moist, gooey treat will envelope you in comfort. Eaten warm, just out of the oven, on a rainy day . . . you'll ache with pleasure!

2	ounces semisweet chocolate, chopped into small pieces
1	cup cake flour
1	teaspoon baking powder
¼	teaspoon salt
½	cup unsalted butter, softened
¾	cup granulated sugar
1	teaspoon ground cloves
½	cup milk, warmed to room temperature
½	cup firmly packed light brown sugar
¼	cup cocoa powder, sifted
1	tablespoon chocolate liqueur
1¼	cups water, boiling

1. Preheat your oven to 350 degrees. Lightly butter an 8-inch square baking pan and dust with flour.
2. Melt the semisweet chocolate, in the top of a double boiler, over hot (not boiling) water, stirring until smooth; remove from heat and cool to tepid.
3. Sift the flour, baking powder, and salt together; set aside.
4. Cream together ¼ cup of the butter and ½ cup of the granulated sugar, with a mixer on high, until fluffy. Adjust to low and slowly add the melted chocolate, cloves, and milk.
5. By hand, using a rubber spatula, blend in the flour mixture. *Don't overmix!* Pour into the prepared pan.
6. Cream together the remaining ¼ cup butter, ¼ cup granulated sugar, brown sugar, cocoa powder, and chocolate liqueur. Add the boiling water and stir until all the ingredients are mixed and melted.
7. Gently spoon the mixture on top of the cake batter, trying not to disturb the batter. DO NOT STIR! (Magically, the sauce will sink to the bottom while the cake bakes!) Bake for 45–55 minutes, until the center is almost firm. Cool on a rack for 15 minutes. Scoop out a spoonful and invert it onto your favorite dessert saucer, so the sauce ends up on top.

Makes 6–8 comforting servings!

Double Chocolate Brownies

Nothing comes close to this cross between a cake and a cookie. For those days when you're aching for rich chocolate in its chewiest form, these are almost as easy as whipping up a package mix and much, much better!

1	cup chopped walnuts	3	eggs, warmed to room temperature
4	ounces semisweet chocolate, chopped into small pieces	½	cup granulated sugar
½	cup unsalted butter, softened	¼	cup firmly packed dark brown sugar
½	cup flour		
¼	teaspoon salt	½	teaspoon vanilla
2	tablespoons cocoa powder, sifted	1	cup (6 ounces) milk chocolate chips

1. Preheat your oven to 350 degrees. Line an 8-inch square baking pan with foil, leaving an overhang. Lightly butter the foil and dust with flour.
2. Toast the walnuts (see "Tips," page xiv); set aside.
3. Melt the semisweet chocolate and butter, in the top of a double boiler, over hot (not boiling) water, stirring until smooth; remove from heat and cool to tepid.
4. Sift together the flour, salt, and cocoa powder; set aside.
5. By hand, whisk the eggs and sugars together. Using a rubber spatula, fold in the vanilla and the chocolate mixture. Fold in the flour mixture, $\frac{1}{4}$ cup at a time, just until dry ingredients are moistened. *Don't overmix!*
6. Spread the batter evenly in the prepared pan. Sprinkle the walnuts and chocolate chips on top. Bake for 25–30 minutes. Lift the foil liner (with the cooked brownies)out of the pan and cool completely on a wire rack.

Makes 16 brownies.

Buttercream Layer Cake

Grandma's layer cake was simply good chocolate cake with sweet, creamy frosting. The only way to improve this American classic is to use rich French or Belgian chocolate!

Chocolate Cake

4 ounces semisweet chocolate, chopped into small pieces
2 cups cake flour
2 teaspoons baking soda
½ teaspoon salt
½ cup unsalted butter, softened
¾ cup granulated sugar
¾ cup firmly packed light brown sugar
3 eggs, warmed to room temperature
2 teaspoons vanilla
½ cup buttermilk, warmed to room temperature
1 cup water, boiling

Buttercream Frosting

2½ cups powdered sugar, sifted
1 cup Dutch-processed (alkalized) cocoa powder
1 cup unsalted butter, softened
1 teaspoon vanilla
1 cup heavy cream, whipped

1. Preheat your oven to 350 degrees. Line the bottom of three 8-inch cake pans with waxed or parchment paper. Lightly butter the paper and sides of the pans and dust with flour.
2. *To make the cake:* Melt the chocolate in the top of a double boiler, over hot (not boiling) water, stirring until smooth; remove from heat and cool to tepid.
3. Sift together the flour, baking soda, and salt; set aside.
4. Cream the butter and sugars together, with a mixer on high, until fluffy. Adjust your mixer to medium and add the eggs, one at a time, and the vanilla. Adjust your mixer to low and blend in the melted chocolate. Continue, alternating the flour mixture (in fourths) and the buttermilk (in thirds). Add the boiling water and beat until the batter is smooth. (The batter will be thin.)
5. Pour the batter into the prepared pans and bake for 25–35 minutes, until a toothpick inserted in the center comes out clean. Cool on wire racks.
6. *To make the buttercream frosting:* Sift together the powdered sugar and cocoa powder; set aside. Cream the butter, with a mixer on high, until fluffy. Add the vanilla. Whip in the sugar mixture, alternately with the cream, until smooth and fluffy.
7. To assemble the cake: Place one 8-inch layer on a dessert platter. Frost the top. Add another layer, frost the top. Add the third layer, frost the top and sides.

Makes 8–10 good old-fashioned servings.

Chocolate Apple Streusel

We confess, Grandma didn't put chocolate in her apple streusel, but our "Apples & Cinnamon" chocolate truffles are so popular, we had to give it a try. See what you think . . .

Cake Batter

4   ounces semisweet chocolate, chopped into small pieces
1½   cups cake flour
2   teaspoons baking powder
½   teaspoon salt
⅓   cup unsalted butter, softened
⅓   cup firmly packed light brown sugar
1   egg, warmed to room temperature
⅓   cup milk, warmed to room temperature

1   teaspoon apple schnapps
1   teaspoon cinnamon schnapps
2   tart apples, chopped in ¼-inch cubes

Streusel Filling

1   cup chopped almonds
½   cup granulated sugar
2   teaspoons ground apple pie spice
2   tablespoons flour
2   tablespoons unsalted butter, chilled

1. Preheat your oven to 400 degrees. Line the bottom of an 8-inch cake pan with waxed or parchment paper. Lightly butter the paper and sides of the pan and dust with flour.

2. *To make the batter:* Melt the chocolate in the top of a double boiler over hot (not boiling) water, stirring until smooth; remove from heat and cool to tepid.

3. Sift together the flour, baking powder, and salt; set aside.

4. Cream the butter and brown sugar together, with a mixer on high, until fluffy. Adjust your mixer to medium and add the egg, schnapps, and milk, one ingredient at a time. Adjust your mixture to low and add the chocolate.

5. By hand, using a rubber spatula, fold in the flour mixture, just until dry ingredients are moistened.

6. *To make the streusel filling:* Toast the almonds (see "Tips," page xiv). Mix the sugar, spice, and flour together. Cut the butter into the sugar mixture, with two knives or a pastry blender, until the mixture has a crumbly texture. Add the almonds, tossing gently.

7. Pour half the batter into the prepared pan. Layer with half the apples and half the streusel filling. Spoon the remaining batter on top, trying not to disturb the filling and top with the remaining apples and streusel filling. Bake for 25–30 minutes. Remove from the oven and cool slightly on a wire rack. Serve warm with butter.

Makes about 8 servings.

Starry Night Muffins

These treats bring two ends of the chocolate spectrum together, contrasting bitter-sweet richness with white chips of sweetness. Make sure you have a cold glass of milk or a hot cup of coffee handy; they're *very* rich!

8	ounces bittersweet chocolate, chopped into small pieces		3	eggs, warmed to room temperature
½	cup unsalted butter, softened		½	cup sugar
1½	cups flour		1½	teaspoons vanilla
¼	cup cocoa powder, sifted		½	cup sour cream, warmed to room temperature
1	teaspoon baking powder			
¾	teaspoon baking soda		1½	cups white chocolate chips
¼	teaspoon salt			(12 ounces)

1. Preheat your oven to 350 degrees and put 12 paper muffin cups into a muffin pan.
2. Melt the bittersweet chocolate and butter in the top of a double boiler over hot (not boiling) water, stirring until smooth; remove from heat and cool to tepid.
3. Sift together the flour, cocoa powder, baking powder, baking soda, and salt; set aside.
4. Beat the eggs and sugar together, with a mixer on high, until fluffy. Adjust your mixer to medium and add the vanilla and sour cream. Adjust your mixer to low and slowly add the chocolate mixture; blend thoroughly.
5. By hand, with a rubber spatula, fold in the flour mixture just until dry ingredients are moistened. *Don't overmix!* Fold in the chocolate chips.
6. Spoon into prepared muffin cups and bake for 15–20 minutes, or until tops spring back when lightly touched. Cool on a wire rack.

Makes 12 muffins.

Chocolate Pound Cake

Grandma's pound cake used a pound of butter and a pound of eggs. We added chocolate to create a simple, yet extremely rich cake. Enjoy it alone or top it with fresh fruit and whipped cream or ice cream!

8	ounces semisweet chocolate, chopped into small pieces	1½	cups sugar
2½	cups flour	1	pound eggs (7 large), warmed to room temperature
1	teaspoon baking powder	1	tablespoon chocolate liqueur
½	teaspoon salt		
1	pound (4 sticks) unsalted butter, softened		

1. Preheat your oven to 350 degrees. Line the bottom of a loaf pan with waxed or parchment paper. Lightly butter the paper and sides of the pan and dust with flour.
2. Melt the chocolate in the top of a double boiler over hot (not boiling) water, stirring until smooth; remove from heat and cool to tepid.
3. Sift together the flour, baking powder, and salt; set aside.
4. Cream together the butter and sugar, with a mixer on high, until fluffy. Adjust your mixer to medium and add the eggs, one at a time, and the liqueur. Adjust your mixer to low and gradually add the chocolate.
5. By hand, with a rubber spatula, fold in the flour mixture, 1/4 cup at a time, just until dry ingredients are moistened. *Don't overmix!*
6. Pour the batter into the prepared pan, tap to remove air bubbles, and level. Bake for an hour, or until a wooden toothpick inserted in the center comes out clean. Cool on a wire rack.

Makes about 12 servings.

Chunky Junkie Bundt

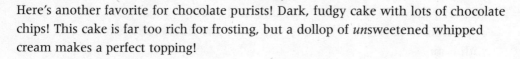

Here's another favorite for chocolate purists! Dark, fudgy cake with lots of chocolate chips! This cake is far too rich for frosting, but a dollop of *un*sweetened whipped cream makes a perfect topping!

6	ounces bittersweet chocolate, chopped
1½	cups flour
⅓	cup cocoa powder, sifted
2	tablespoons instant espresso powder
1	teaspoon baking soda
½	teaspoon salt
½	cup unsalted butter, warmed to room temperature
4	ounces cream cheese, warmed to room temperature
1	cup granulated sugar
½	cup firmly packed light brown sugar
2	eggs, warmed to room temperature
1	cup half & half, warmed to room temperature
12	ounces semisweet chocolate chips
2	tablespoons powdered sugar, sifted

1. Preheat your oven to 350 degrees. Lightly butter the inside of a bundt pan and dust with flour.
2. Melt the chocolate in the top of a double boiler over hot (not boiling) water, stirring until smooth; remove from heat and cool to tepid.
3. Sift together the flour, cocoa powder, espresso powder, baking soda, and salt; set aside.
4. Cream together the butter, cheese, and sugars, with a mixer on a high. Adjust your mixer to medium and add the eggs, one at a time, and the half & half, beating thoroughly after each addition. Adjust your mixer to low and gradually add the melted chocolate.
5. By hand, using a rubber spatula, fold in the flour mixture and the chocolate chips. *Don't overmix!*
6. Pour the batter into the bundt pan and bake for 45 minutes or until a wooden toothpick inserted in the center comes out clean. Cool on a wire rack. Transfer to your favorite cake plate and dust with powdered sugar.

Makes 10–12 achingly rich slices.

Cocoa Butter Cookies

For Chocolate Days around the holidays, try these little cookie-press treats! Whimsical chocolate snowmen, chocolate shamrocks, chocolate pumpkins . . . can't help but put a smile on your face!

4 ounces milk chocolate, chopped into small pieces	1 cup unsalted butter, softened
2½ cups flour	¾ cup sugar
½ teaspoon baking powder	1 egg, warmed to room temperature
¼ teaspoon salt	Toppings (candied fruit, nuts, sprinkles, etc.)

1. Preheat your oven to 375 degrees. Cover cookie sheets with parchment paper.
2. Melt the chocolate in the top of a double boiler over hot (not boiling) water, stirring until smooth; remove from heat and cool to tepid.
3. Sift together the flour, baking powder, and salt; set aside.
4. Cream together the butter and sugar, with a mixer on high, until fluffy. Adjust your mixer to medium and add the egg. Adjust your mixer to low and gradually add the melted chocolate.
5. By hand, using a rubber spatula, fold in the flour mixture, just until the dry ingredients are moistened. *Don't overmix!*
6. Chill the dough for 30 minutes and feed through a cookie-press. Bake the cookies for 8–10 minutes and decorate with your favorite toppings.

Makes about 4 dozen cocoa cuties.

Guilt-Free Days

On those days when, even though you've adopted a healthier diet, you get an overwhelming desire for chocolate, you can still follow your instincts. For, much like a baked potato, if you partner your favorite form of chocolate with reduced-fat ingredients, you can enjoy a wide variety of tasty treats. In fact, you'll find that by transforming old favorites to healthier standards, you've created new guilt-free desserts that are even more delicious!

Mocha L'Orange Slush

If you loved slurpees as a child, you'll love this grown-up version of that icy, slushy treat!

1	ounce bittersweet chocolate, chopped into small pieces	3	tablespoons light brown sugar
½	cup lowfat milk (1%)	1	teaspoon instant espresso powder
½	cup brewed coffee	½	teaspoon cinnamon
2	tablespoons Dutch-processed cocoa powder (alkalized)	3	drops orange oil
			Orange zest for garnish

1. Place the chocolate in a mixing bowl; set aside.
2. In a heavy-bottomed saucepan, combine all but two tablespoons *each* of the milk and coffee, with the cocoa, sugar, espresso powder, cinnamon, and orange oil. Heat, stirring until the sugar is melted. Pour over the chopped chocolate and stir until completely melted and smooth.
3. Pour this mocha mixture into miniature ice cube trays and freeze.
4. Pop the frozen cubes in your blender with the remaining 2 tablespoons *each* of the milk and coffee. Pulsate into slush, pour into an iced Irish coffee mug, and top with the orange zest.

Makes one sophisticated slush.

Angel Berry Trifle

This treat looks as beautiful as it tastes and brings together layers of naturally lowfat, sweet, and tangy treats.

¾	cup cake flour	1	teaspoon vanilla
¼	cup cocoa powder	½	cup strawberry sorbet
1¼	cups egg whites (8–9), warmed to room temperature	½	cup chocolate frozen yogurt
¾	teaspoon cream of tartar	¼	cup sliced strawberries
⅛	teaspoon salt	¼	cup blackberries
1½	cups superfine sugar	¼	cup raspberries
		1	sprig of fresh mint

1. Preheat your oven to 375 degrees. Make sure your angel cake pan is clean and dry. Cover the bottom of the pan with waxed or parchment paper. DO NOT butter or grease it.
2. Sift the flour and cocoa powder together until evenly mixed.
3. Beat the egg whites, with a mixer on medium, until foamy. Adjust mixer to high and continue to whip, adding the cream of tartar and salt. When soft peaks form, gradually add the sugar and continue to whip until stiff peaks form.
4. By hand, with a rubber spatula, gently fold the vanilla into the egg whites. In small increments, sprinkle the flour mixture into the egg whites and gently fold, taking care not to overmix or deflate the egg whites!
5. Gently push the batter into prepared loaf pan. Carefully cut through the batter with your spatula to remove air bubbles, then gently level the top. Bake for 35–40 minutes on the lower rack. Invert pan onto wire racks and cool completely. Cut into bite-size cubes.
6. *To assemble the trifle:* In the bottom of a parfait glass or miniature trifle bowl, spoon a small amount of sorbet. Add a layer of angel cake cubes. Top with a small amount of frozen yogurt, strawberries, and sorbet. Layer, in order, the angel cake cubes, frozen yogurt, blackberries, and sorbet. Top with remaining angel cake cubes, the rest of the frozen yogurt, raspberries, and a sprig of fresh mint.

Makes one heavenly serving.

Banana Fudge Muffins

If you wake up aching for chocolate, these tasty breakfast snacks will provide you with all the essentials; fruit, bran, yogurt, and, best of all, chocolate!

4	ounces semisweet chocolate, chopped into small pieces
2	tablespoons butter
½	cup all-purpose flour
½	cup wheat flour
¼	cup oat bran
¼	cup cocoa powder
1½	teaspoons baking powder
1	teaspoon baking soda
¼	teaspoon salt

1	egg, warmed to room temperature
1	egg white, warmed to room temperature
⅓	cup honey
2	tablespoons canola oil
½	cup plain yogurt, warmed to room temperature
1	cup mashed bananas (about 2 medium)
½	cup chopped cashews

1. Preheat your oven to 400 degrees and place 12 paper cups in a muffin pan.
2. Melt the chocolate in the top of a double boiler, over hot (not boiling) water. Brown the butter in a small saucepan and add to the chocolate, stirring until smooth; remove from heat and cool to tepid.
3. Sift together the flours, bran, cocoa powder, baking powder, baking soda, and salt; set aside.
4. Beat the egg and egg white, with a mixer on high, until fluffy. Adjust your mixer to medium and blend in the honey, oil, and yogurt. Adjust your mixer to low and gradually add the chocolate mixture.
5. By hand, with a rubber spatula, fold in the flour mixture, just until dry ingredients are moistened. *Don't overmix!* Fold in bananas and cashews. Spoon into muffin cups and bake for 18–20 minutes, or until a wooden toothpick inserted in the center comes out clean. Try to let them cool, just a little!

Makes 12 healthy muffins.

IcedWiches

Are ice cream sandwiches (chocolate, vanilla, and strawberry ice cream, sandwiched between two chewy chocolate cookies) what you crave on your Chocolate Days? Try this reduced-fat version. It's even better!

Meringue Wafers

²⁄₃	cup superfine sugar
2½	tablespoons cocoa powder, sifted
3	egg whites, warmed to room temperature
¼	teaspoon cream of tartar

Iced Milks

12	ounces bittersweet chocolate, chopped into small pieces
2	cups water
1	cup skim milk
1¾	cups superfine sugar
1	tablespoon chocolate liqueur
1	tablespoon instant espresso powder
1	tablespoon coffee liqueur
1	tablespoon seedless raspberry preserves
1	tablespoon raspberry liqueur

1. Preheat your oven to 200 degrees. Cover cookie sheets with parchment paper.
2. *To make the meringue wafers:* Sift together the sugar and cocoa powder; set aside.

3. Beat the egg whites, with a mixer on medium, until foamy. Adjust your mixer to high and beat, adding cream of tartar, until soft peaks form. Gradually add the sugar mixture, until stiff peaks form.
4. Use a spoon or fill a pastry bag, fitted with a medium star tip and pipe ½-inch-thick round wafers, about 3 inches in diameter. Bake for 30 minutes. Turn your oven off and leave the disks in the oven until completely cool.
5. *To make the iced milks:* Place the chocolate in a bowl; set aside. In a heavy-bottomed saucepan bring the water, milk, and sugar to a simmer over medium heat, stirring until the sugar is completely melted. Pour over the chocolate, stirring until smooth. Separate evenly into three freezer bowls.
6. In one, add the chocolate liqueur, and mix thoroughly. In another, add the espresso powder and coffee liqueur, and mix thoroughly. In the third, add the raspberry preserves and liqueur, and mix thoroughly. Freeze all three, stirring from time to time to break up the sugar crystals.
7. *To assemble:* Place one small scoop of each iced milk between two meringue wafers.

Makes 8–10 IcedWiches.

Irish Cream Cheese Cups

These crustless, individual cheesecakes are both light and rich. And, laced with one of the new "light" Irish Cream liqueurs, they're truly extravagant!

2 ounces white chocolate, chopped into small pieces

1 tablespoon flour

2 tablespoons cocoa powder

½ cup superfine sugar

⅛ teaspoon salt

¼ cup lowfat cottage cheese, warmed to room temperature

¼ cup lowfat sour cream, warmed to room temperature

8 ounces Neufchâtel cheese, warmed to room temperature

1 egg, warmed to room temperature

2 egg whites, warmed to room temperature

5 to 6 tablespoons "light" Irish Cream liqueur

1. Preheat your oven to 350 degrees. Place 4–6 custard cups in a baking pan.
2. Microwave the white chocolate, on a MEDIUM setting, for 10 seconds. Stir thoroughly. Repeat, heating for only 10 seconds at a time, until completely melted; set aside to cool to tepid.
3. Sift together the flour, cocoa powder, sugar, and salt; set aside.
4. Blend the cottage cheese in your food processor or blender until smooth. Add the sour cream, Neufchâtel, egg, egg whites, flour mixture, melted chocolate, and 1 tablespoon liqueur, one ingredient at a time; blend, just until smooth, with a pulsating action.
5. Divide the batter among the custard cups. Pour hot water into the baking pan, in which the cups are sitting, so that it comes halfway up the sides of the cups and bake, on the lower rack of your oven, for 25–30 minutes. (The centers will not be firm.) Remove the cups from the baking pan, cool on a wire rack, and refrigerate for at least 8 hours. Unmold your guilt-free treats and lace each with 1 tablespoon of "light" Irish Cream liqueur!

Makes 4–6 elegant indulgences.

CocoLocos

These crazy little chocolate, oat, and candied-fruit cookies are great to take along on road trips, shopping sprees, and skating runs for instant healthy energy!

⅔	cup flour	¼	cup canola oil
½	cup cocoa powder	2	egg whites, warmed to room temperature
1	teaspoon baking powder		
½	teaspoon salt	⅓	cup lowfat milk (1%), warmed to room temperature
2	tablespoons unsalted butter, softened		
		1	teaspoon vanilla
½	cup firmly packed dark brown sugar	2	cups oats, uncooked
		1	cup candied fruit bits
½	cup granulated sugar		

1. Preheat your oven to 375 degrees. Use nonstick cookie sheets or lightly spray aluminum sheets with canola oil.
2. Sift together the flour, cocoa powder, baking powder, and salt; set aside.
3. Cream together the butter and sugars, with a mixer on high, until fluffy. Adjust your mixer to medium and add the oil, egg whites, milk, and vanilla, one ingredient at a time, blending thoroughly.
4. By hand, using a rubber spatula, fold in the flour mixture, just until the dry ingredients are moistened. *Don't overmix!* Fold in the oats, $\frac{1}{2}$ cup at a time, and the candied fruit, $\frac{1}{4}$ cup at a time.
5. Drop by rounded teaspoonfuls on prepared sheets and bake for 10 minutes. Cool on wire racks.

Makes about 36 cookies.

CappCakes

If you love rich cappuccino, try these espresso-laced cupcakes. They're great for a mid-morning or afternoon boost, especially at the office!

2	ounces bittersweet chocolate, chopped into small pieces	¼	cup canola oil
1¼	cups flour	1	egg, warmed to room temperature
⅓	cup cocoa powder	2	egg whites, warmed to room temperature
1	teaspoon baking powder	¼	cup brewed coffee, cooled to tepid
½	teaspoon baking soda	2	tablespoons instant espresso
¼	teaspoon salt	1	teaspoon coffee liqueur
2	tablespoons unsalted butter, softened	¼	cup lowfat milk (1%), warmed to room temperature
½	cup firmly packed light brown sugar	2	tablespoons powdered, sweetened chocolate
½	cup granulated sugar		

1. Preheat your oven to 350 degrees. Put 12 paper cups in a cupcake pan.
2. Microwave the bittersweet chocolate, on a MEDIUM setting, for 10 seconds. Stir thoroughly. Repeat, heating for only 10 seconds at a time, until completely melted; set aside to cool to tepid.
3. Sift together the flour, cocoa powder, baking powder, baking soda, and salt; set aside.
4. Cream together the butter and sugars, using a mixer on high, until fluffy. Adjust your mixer to medium and add the oil, egg, and egg whites, one at a time. Adjust your mixer to low and slowly add the melted chocolate, coffee, instant espresso, liqueur, and milk.
5. By hand, using a rubber spatula, fold in the flour mixture, just until completely blended and smooth. *Don't overmix!*
6. Spoon the batter into prepared cups and bake for 25–30 minutes, or until tops spring back when lightly touched. Cool on wire racks and dust with powdered chocolate.

Makes 12 CappCakes.

Chocolate Ecstasy!

What would you call a new chocolate dessert that actually tastes better than your favorite decadent torte *and* reduces much of its fat? Sheer Chocolate Ecstasy!

¼	cup skinned almonds	2	egg yolks, warmed to room temperature
1	tablespoon unsalted butter		
4	ounces Neufchâtel cheese, warmed to room temperature	½	cup granulated sugar
		3	tablespoons flour
½	cup cocoa powder, sifted	3	egg whites, warmed to room temperature
4	ounces semisweet chocolate, chopped into small pieces		
		¼	teaspoon cream of tartar
⅓	cup water, boiling	¼	cup superfine sugar
1	tablespoon amaretto liqueur	1	tablespoon powdered sugar

1. Toast and grind the almonds (see "Tips," page xiv).
2. Preheat oven to 375 degrees. Cover the bottom of an 8-inch springform pan with parchment paper and lightly spray the paper and sides of the pan with canola oil.
3. In a heavy-bottomed saucepan, brown the butter. Remove the pan from the heat and, by hand, whisk in the cheese, cocoa powder, and chopped chocolate. Add the water and whisk until all ingredients are thoroughly melted. Add the liqueur, mix thoroughly; set aside to cool to tepid.

4. Beat the egg yolks and granulated sugar, with a mixer on medium, until thick.
5. By hand, whisk $\frac{1}{4}$ of the egg mixture into the chocolate mixture. Switch, and gradually whisk the chocolate mixture into the egg mixture. With a rubber spatula, gently fold the flour and nuts into the chocolate mixture. *Don't overmix*; set aside.
6. In a clean, dry bowl beat the egg whites with a mixer on medium, until foamy. Adjust your mixer to high and continue to beat, adding the cream of tartar. When soft peaks form, gradually add the superfine sugar, beating until stiff peaks form.
7. Gently fold $\frac{1}{4}$ of the egg whites into the chocolate mixture; continue in three more increments. *Don't overmix!*
8. Pour the batter into the prepared pan and place on the lower rack of the oven. Bake for approximately 30 minutes, until the top springs back when lightly touched. Cool the torte completely on a wire rack, transfer to your favorite dessert platter, and dust with powdered sugar.

Makes 16 heart-smart wedges.

Chocolate Mint Clouds

Lighter than air, these bite-sized meringues are simple to make, and are perfect when all you need are little bits of chocolate!

3 egg whites, warmed to room temperature
⅛ teaspoon cream of tartar
⅔ cup superfine sugar

½ teaspoon peppermint extract
¼ cup semisweet mint chocolate chips

1. Preheat oven to 275 degrees. Use nonstick cookie sheets or cover aluminum sheets with parchment paper.
2. Beat the egg whites, with a mixer on medium, until foamy. Adjust your mixer to high and sprinkle in the cream of tartar while beating. When soft peaks form, sprinkle in the sugar, a tablespoon at a time, beating until stiff peaks form. Drizzle in the peppermint extract and beat for just a second or two more.
3. By hand, with a rubber spatula, gently fold in the chocolate chips, taking care not to deflate the egg whites.
4. Drop by teaspoonfuls onto cookie sheets. Bake for one hour. Turn your oven off and leave the cookies inside to cool for another hour.

Makes 4–5 dozen bite-sized puffs.

Sticky-Sweet Days

Do you ache for those Chocolate Days when birthday parties meant cookies, cakes, and buttercream frosting so sweet your parents had to peel you off the ceiling? That sugar rush can be yours again in new combinations of favorite flavors. For these treats we started with the naturally sweeter white and milk chocolates and let ourselves get carried away with fun and fancy!

Rainbow Crispies

What could be better than everyone's favorite crispy rice cereal cookies? How about *chocolate* rice cereal cookies, slathered with marshmallow frosting and sprinkled with a rainbow of miniature M & M's!

Crispy Cookie

¼   cup unsalted butter, softened
40 marshmallows
5   cups chocolate rice cereal

Marshmallow Frosting

2   egg whites, warmed to room
    temperature
6   tablespoons powdered sugar
2   tablespoons light corn syrup
1   teaspoon vanilla
½   cup miniature M & M's

1. Line an 8-inch square baking pan with waxed paper.
2. *To make the cookies:* melt the butter and marshmallows in a large saucepan over low heat, stirring until completely melted. Remove from heat and gently fold in the cereal. Spread into the prepared pan and cool.
3. *To make the frosting:* Place the egg whites, sugar, and corn syrup in the top of a double boiler, over boiling water. Beat, with a mixer on high, until soft peaks form. Remove from the heat, add the vanilla, and continue to beat for another minute.
4. Remove the cookies from the pan. Spread with the frosting, and top with M & M's.

Makes 16 squares.

Liar's Dice

When your Chocolate Day puts you in the mood to gamble, try these *white* chocolate brownies for a change! And just for fun, frost them with Irish Creme-laced chocolate and decorate them with chocolate chips in dice patterns!

Brownies

4	ounces white chocolate, chopped into small pieces
6	tablespoons unsalted butter, softened
¾	cup flour
½	teaspoon baking powder
¼	teaspoon salt
2	eggs, warmed to room temperature
⅓	cup granulated sugar
⅓	cup firmly packed light brown sugar
1	teaspoon vanilla

Frosting

8	ounces white chocolate, chopped into small pieces
2	tablespoons unsalted butter, softened
1	tablespoon heavy cream
1	tablespoon Irish Cream liqueur
¼	cup semisweet, mini-morsel, chocolate chips

1. Preheat your oven to 350 degrees and line an 8-inch square baking pan with foil, leaving an overhang. Lightly butter the foil and dust with flour.
2. *To make the brownies:* Melt the white chocolate and butter in the top of a double boiler, over hot (not boiling) water, stirring until smooth; remove from heat and cool to tepid.
3. Sift together the flour, baking powder, and salt; set aside.
4. Beat the eggs and sugars, with a mixer on medium, until fluffy. Add the vanilla and beat until thoroughly blended. Adjust your mixer to low and slowly add the chocolate mixture.
5. By hand, using a rubber spatula, fold in the flour mixture, just until the dry ingredients are moistened.
6. Pour the batter into the prepared pan and bake for 20–25 minutes. Lift the foil liner, with the brownies, out of the pan and cool thoroughly on a wire rack.
7. *To make the frosting:* Melt the white chocolate, butter, and cream in the top of a double boiler, over hot (not boiling) water, stirring until smooth; remove from the heat, stir in the liqueur, and cool to tepid.
8. *To top the brownies:* Spread the frosting over the cooled brownies and allow the frosting to cool completely before carefully cutting them into 1-inch squares. Now, (this is the fun part) gently press the peaked side of the mini-chips into the frosted brownies in dice patterns.

Makes 64, 1-inch boxcars, Little Joes, snake eyes . . .

Banana Split Trifle

Here's an old-fashioned sweet treat, updated and sophisticated, for those Chocolate Days when you'd love to wander down to a soda fountain and dive into an achingly delicious banana split!

6	ounces milk chocolate, chopped into small pieces	1½	cups thinly sliced bananas
6	eggs, separated and warmed to room temperature	1½	cups thinly sliced strawberries
2	teaspoons vanilla	1½	cups chocolate fudge topping
¾	cup flour	1	cup (6 ounces) butterscotch chips
½	cup dry roasted peanuts	1	cup miniature marshmallows
¼	cup unsalted butter, softened	2	cups strawberry ice cream, in small scoops
¼	teaspoon cream of tartar	2	cups vanilla ice cream, in small scoops
¼	cup superfine sugar		Whipped cream
2	cups chocolate ice cream, in small scoops		Maraschino cherries

1. Preheat your oven to 350 degrees. Line the bottom of an 11 × 17-inch pan with waxed or parchment paper. Lightly butter the paper and sides of the pan and dust with flour.
2. Melt the chocolate in the top of a double boiler, over hot (not boiling) water, stirring until smooth; remove from heat and cool to tepid.
3. Beat the egg yolks and vanilla, with a mixer on medium, until thick; set aside.
4. Pulsate the flour and nuts together in your food processor or blender, until the nuts are a fine powder; set aside.

5. Cream the butter, with a mixer on high, until fluffy. Adjust your mixer to medium and slowly add the egg yolk mixture. Adjust your mixer to low and add the melted chocolate.

6. By hand, using a rubber spatula, fold in the flour mixture, until dry ingredients are moistened. *Don't overmix!*

7. Beat the egg whites, with a mixer on medium until foamy. Adjust mixer to high and continue to beat, sprinkling in the cream of tartar. When soft peaks begin to form, sprinkle in the sugar and beat until stiff peaks form. By hand, using a rubber spatula, gently fold $\frac{1}{4}$ of the egg whites into the batter. Quickly fold in the remaining egg whites, in three more increments. *Don't overmix!*

8. Spread the batter evenly into your prepared pan. Bake for 30 minutes, until the cake springs back when lightly touched. Remove from the pan and cool on wire racks. When completely cool, trim the edges and cut into cubes.

9. Cover the bottom of your trifle bowl with $\frac{1}{3}$ of the cake cubes. Layer with the chocolate ice cream, $\frac{1}{2}$ cup bananas, $\frac{1}{2}$ cup strawberries, $\frac{1}{2}$ cup fudge topping, $\frac{1}{3}$ cup butterscotch chips, and $\frac{1}{3}$ cup marshmallows. Top with $\frac{1}{2}$ the remaining cake cubes, the strawberry ice cream, $\frac{1}{2}$ cup bananas, $\frac{1}{2}$ cup strawberries, $\frac{1}{2}$ cup fudge topping, $\frac{1}{3}$ cup butterscotch chips, and $\frac{1}{3}$ cup marshmallows. Top with the remaining cake cubes, the vanilla ice cream, and the remaining bananas, strawberries, fudge topping, butterscotch chips, and marshmallows. Top each individual serving with a dollop of whipped cream and a maraschino cherry.

Makes 6–8 soda shop servings.

Macadamia Macaroons

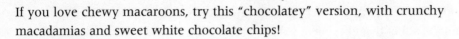

If you love chewy macaroons, try this "chocolatey" version, with crunchy macadamias and sweet white chocolate chips!

6 ounces milk chocolate, chopped into small pieces
1 egg, separated and warmed to room temperature
1 teaspoon vanilla
1 egg white, warmed to room temperature

⅛ teaspoon cream of tartar
⅓ cup superfine sugar
1 cup flaked coconut
1 cup macadamia nuts, chopped
1 cup white chocolate chips (6 ounces)

1. Preheat your oven to 325 degrees. Use nonstick cookie sheets or cover sheets with parchment paper.
2. Melt the milk chocolate, in the top of a double boiler, over hot (not boiling) water, stirring until smooth; remove from heat and cool to tepid. Whisk in the egg yolk and vanilla; set aside.
3. Beat the egg whites, with a mixer on medium until foamy. Adjust your mixer to high and continue to beat, sprinkling in the cream of tartar. When soft peaks form, sprinkle in the sugar, one tablespoon at a time, and beat until stiff peaks form; set aside.
4. By hand, with a rubber spatula, gently fold $\frac{1}{4}$ of the egg whites into the chocolate mixture. Fold in the remaining egg whites, in three more increments. Carefully fold in the coconut, nuts, and chips. *Don't overmix!*
5. Drop teaspoonfuls onto the prepared cookie sheets and bake for 18 minutes. Cool on wire racks.

Makes about 48 chewy treats.

Chocolate Pizza

When everyone you know is having a Chocolate Day, have a pizza party! Ask each of your friends to bring their favorite topping and see how many different combinations you can create!

12 ounces milk chocolate, chopped into small pieces

½ cup plus 2 tablespoons unsalted butter, softened

2 eggs, warmed to room temperature

⅓ cup firmly packed dark brown sugar

1 cup flour

¼ teaspoon salt

8 ounces cream cheese, softened

½ cup powdered sugar

¼ cup heavy cream, warmed to room temperature

Toppings! (chocolate chips, nuts, fruit, marshmallows, sundae toppings, bits of candy, cookies . . .)

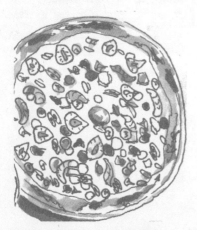

1. Preheat oven to 350 degrees. Lightly butter the bottom of a 12-inch pizza pan and dust with flour.
2. Melt the chocolate and ½ cup of the butter in the top of a double boiler, over hot (not boiling) water, stirring until smooth; remove from heat and cool to tepid.
3. Beat the eggs, with a mixer on medium, until fluffy. Gradually beat in the brown sugar. Adjust your mixer to low and slowly add the chocolate mixture.
4. By hand, using a rubber spatula, fold in the flour and salt.
5. Spread the batter into the prepared pan. Bake for 15 to 18 minutes and place on wire racks to cool.
6. Cream the cheese, 2 tablespoons butter, and powdered sugar, with a mixer on high, until fluffy. Adjust your mixer to low and slowly mix in the heavy cream. Spread on the cooling pizza and top with . . . you name it!

Makes about 8 slices.

Lemon Cream Dreams

These sweet, white chocolate cupcakes have a creamy surprise in the center!

Chocolate Cupcakes

4	ounces white chocolate, chopped into small pieces
½	cup heavy cream
1¾	cups flour
1	teaspoon baking soda
⅛	teaspoon salt
½	cup unsalted butter, softened
4	ounces cream cheese, softened
1	cup granulated sugar
1	teaspoon vanilla
3	eggs, warmed to room temperature

Lemon Buttercream Frosting

½	cup unsalted butter, softened
½	cup powdered sugar, sifted
½	cup heavy cream
⅛	teaspoon lemon oil
12	maraschino cherries

1. Preheat your oven to 350 degrees. Put 12 paper cups in a cupcake pan.
2. *To make the cupcakes:* Melt the chocolate and cream in the top of a double boiler, over hot (not boiling) water, stirring until smooth; remove from heat and cool to tepid.

3. Sift together the flour, baking soda, and salt; set aside.
4. Cream together the butter, cheese, sugar, and vanilla, with a mixer on high, until fluffy. Adjust your mixer to medium and add the eggs, one at a time, mixing thoroughly after each addition. Adjust your mixer to low and slowly add the chocolate mixture.
5. By hand, with a rubber spatula, fold in the flour mixture, ¼ cup at a time, just until dry ingredients are moistened. *Don't overmix!*
6. Spoon into the prepared cups and bake for 15 minutes or until the top springs back when lightly touched. Cool on wire racks.
7. *To make the frosting:* Whip the butter and sugar, with a mixer on high, until fluffy. Continue to beat, adding the cream and lemon oil.
8. Fill a pastry bag, fitted with a star tip, and gently push the tip into the top of each cupcake, squeezing a bit of cream into the center. Decorate the top of each cupcake with the remaining frosting and a maraschino cherry.

Makes 12 creamy cupcakes.

Tri-Chocolate Pie

Dark, sweet cookie crumbs hold a layer of rich milk chocolate cheesecake and a fluffy white chocolate crown!

Chocolate Crumb Crust

4   cups plus 2 tablespoons chocolate cookie crumbs (1 pound package)
¼   cup superfine sugar
½   cup unsalted butter, melted

Milk Chocolate Cheesecake

5   ounces milk chocolate, chopped into small pieces
8   ounces cream cheese, softened
⅓   cup superfine sugar
1   teaspoon vanilla
1   egg, warmed to room temperature

White Chocolate Crown

4   ounces white chocolate, chopped into small pieces
6   ounces cream cheese, softened
½   cup superfine sugar
1   teaspoon vanilla
½   cup heavy cream, at room temperature
1   cup heavy cream, whipped

1. *To make the chocolate crumb crust:* Preheat your oven to 450 degrees. Line the bottom of a 9-inch springform pan with waxed or parchment paper. Lightly butter the paper and sides of the pan and dust with flour.

2. Combine 4 cups cookie crumbs, sugar, and butter in a mixing bowl. Press the mixture onto the bottom and sides of the prepared pan. Bake for 5 minutes and allow to cool completely, on a wire rack, before filling. Turn your oven down to 350 degrees.

3. *To make the milk chocolate cheesecake:* Melt the milk chocolate in a double boiler, over hot (not boiling) water, stirring until smooth; remove from heat and cool to tepid.

4. Cream the cheese, using a mixer on high, until fluffy. Add the sugar, vanilla, and egg, one ingredient at a time, beating until smooth after each addition. Adjust your mixer to low and slowly add the melted chocolate. Pour into your cooled crust and bake for 40–45 minutes. (The center will still be soft.) Turn your oven off and allow the cheesecake to cool in the oven one hour.

5. *To make the white chocolate crown:* Melt the white chocolate in a double boiler, over hot (not boiling) water, stirring until smooth; remove from heat and cool to tepid.

6. Cream together the cheese, sugar, vanilla, and the ½ cup of room temperature heavy cream, with a mixer on high; beat until fluffy.

7. By hand, using a rubber spatula, gently fold the melted chocolate and whipped cream into the whipped cream and cheese mixture, taking care not to deflate the cheese mixture. Spoon onto the top of the cooled cheesecake. Sprinkle the remaining 2 tablespoons cookie crumbs on top and refrigerate.

Makes 8–12 servings.

Peanut Butter Cup Cakes

Do you crave peanut butter cups on your Chocolate Days? Try "streuseling" them between chocolate and peanut butter cakes topped with a sugary, peanut butter-cream frosting!

Chocolate Peanut Butter Cupcakes

4   ounces milk chocolate, chopped into small pieces
2   cups flour
1   teaspoon baking powder
¼   teaspoon salt
1   cup unsalted butter, softened
¾   cup granulated sugar
¾   cup firmly packed light brown sugar
5   eggs, warmed to room temperature
½   cup creamy peanut butter
½   cup buttermilk, warmed to room temperature
12 Reese's peanut butter cup miniatures (9 ounce package)

Peanut Buttercream Frosting

¼   cup unsalted butter, softened
¼   cup creamy peanut butter
½   cup powdered sugar, sifted
½   cup heavy cream

1. Preheat your oven to 350 degrees. Put 12 paper cups in a cupcake pan.
2. *To make the cupcakes:* Melt the chocolate in the top of a double boiler, over hot (not boiling) water, stirring until smooth; remove from heat and cool to tepid.

3. Sift together the flour, baking powder, and salt.

4. Cream together the butter and sugars, with a mixer on high, until fluffy. Adjust your mixer to medium and add the eggs, one at a time, beating thoroughly after each. Split the batter into two bowls. Adjust your mixture to low and, in one bowl, blend in the melted chocolate. In the other, blend in the peanut butter.

5. By hand, using a rubber spatula, fold half the flour mixture into the chocolate batter, in $\frac{1}{4}$ cup increments, alternating with $\frac{1}{4}$ cup of the buttermilk, in 2 tablespoon increments, just until blended. *Don't overmix!* Fold the remaining flour mixture into the peanut butter batter, alternating with the remaining $\frac{1}{4}$ cup buttermilk.

6. Spoon the chocolate batter into the prepared paper cups. Break up a peanut butter cup in each, forming a "streusel" layer. Carefully spoon the peanut butter batter on top, trying not to disturb the peanut butter cup filling. Bake for 40–45 minutes, until the top springs back when lightly touched. Cool on wire racks.

7. *To make the frosting:* Whip the butter, peanut butter, and sugar, with a mixer on high, until fluffy. Continue to beat, adding the cream. Frost the cooled cupcakes.

Makes 12 "cup" cakes.

Peaches and Cream Truffles

If you've not yet tried white chocolate, let these bite-size sweeties be your introduction; they'll steal your heart and melt you into cocoa blanc bliss!

8	ounces white chocolate, chopped into small pieces	1	tablespoon Irish Cream liqueur
3	tablespoons heavy cream	12	ounces white chocolate, tempered (see "Tips," page xiii)
1	tablespoon peach preserves	¼	cup shaved white chocolate

1. Place the chopped chocolate in a mixing bowl.
2. In a heavy-bottomed saucepan, bring the cream to a simmer, three times. removing the pan from the heat for a few seconds between simmers. Pour over the chopped chocolate and allow to stand for 1 minute. Stir until smooth. Add the preserves and liqueur and mix thoroughly. Cover and refrigerate.

3. When fairly solid, scoop out teaspoonfuls and roll into balls. Cover a cookie sheet with waxed paper. With the tempered chocolate, make $\frac{1}{4}$-inch chocolate spots on the waxed paper, $1\frac{1}{2}$ inches apart; allow to cool. With a spiral dipping fork (see *note*), dip the truffles in 107 degree tempered chocolate and place atop each spot of chocolate. (The heavy ganache tends to sink, so the spots create solid bottoms and help seal the truffles.) Top each immediately with shaved chocolate and cool. Serve in petit four-sized cups.

Note: Spiral dipping forks are available at most specialty baking stores, or you can use a regular fork bent at a right angle (similar to the shape of an Easter egg dipper).

Makes about 20 truffles.

Ultrarich Days

For those Chocolate Days when you'd rather be relaxing in an exclusive patisserie just off the Champs-Elysees, we've created sophisticated pamperings which blend dark, rich bittersweet and semi-sweet chocolates with flavors the grown-up in you savors. Fresh tart raspberries, musky roasted hazelnuts, and French cognac are only a few of the simple yet elegant ingredients that enhance these world-class chocolate desserts.

Raspberry Crowns

These elegant, bite-size, chocolate tortes crowned with rich Italian cream cheese and fresh, succulent berries will make you feel like royalty!

12	ounces semisweet chocolate, chopped into small pieces	¼	cup granulated sugar
6	tablespoons unsalted butter, softened	2	tablespoons flour
1	tablespoon, plus 8 teaspoons Chambord liqueur	⅓	cup mascarpone cheese, softened
1	tablespoon seedless raspberry preserves	2	tablespoons powdered sugar
4	eggs, warmed to room temperature	1	tablespoon Dutch-processed cocoa powder (alkalized)
		24	fresh raspberries, washed and gently patted dry

1. Preheat your oven to 425 degrees. Line the bottom of a 9-inch springform pan with waxed or parchment paper. Lightly butter the paper and sides of the pan and dust with flour.

2. Melt the chocolate and butter in the top of a double boiler, over hot (not boiling) water, stirring until smooth; remove from heat and cool to tepid. In a separate bowl, blend one tablespoon of the liqueur and the preserves together and add to the chocolate mixture, stirring until smooth.

3. Beat the eggs, with a mixer on high, until fluffy. Add the granulated sugar. Mix thoroughly.

4. By hand, using a rubber spatula, fold the flour into the egg mixture. Gently fold ¼ of the egg mixture into the chocolate mixture. Switch, gently folding ¼ of the chocolate mixture into the egg mixture, taking care not to deflate the egg mixture. Continue folding the chocolate mixture into the egg mixture in three more increments. *Don't overmix!*

5. Pour the batter into the pan, level the top, and bake for 15 minutes. Let cool to room temperature on a wire rack. Remove from pan to a flat working surface. Using a 2-inch cookie cutter, cut 8 circles out of the torte.

6. Cream together the cheese, powdered sugar, and cocoa. Place in a pastry bag fitted with a star tip. Decorate the top of each circle with three stars, and place a fresh raspberry, top side down, in the center of each star. Cover and refrigerate or serve, at room temperature, on your favorite dessert plates which have each been lightly laced with 1 teaspoon of Chambord liqueur.

Makes 8 crowns plus leftover bits.

Bittersweet Crème Brûlée

Chunks of bittersweet chocolate contrast in texture with the smooth egg custard and in taste with the sweet caramelized sugar topping!

2½ cups heavy cream

¼ cup plus 4 tablespoons superfine sugar

4 large egg yolks, warmed to room temperature

½ teaspoon vanilla

4 ounces bittersweet chocolate, chopped into chunks

1. Preheat your oven to 350 degrees. Place 4 ramekins in a baking pan.
2. In the top of a double boiler, heat the cream and ¼ cup of the sugar, over simmering water, stirring until the sugar is dissolved; remove from heat and cool to tepid.
3. Whisk the egg yolks and vanilla together. Slowly, add the cream mixture and continue whisking until thoroughly mixed. Fold in the chocolate chunks.
4. Spoon into the ramekins and pour hot water into the baking pan so that the water comes halfway up the sides of the ramekins. Bake for 45–50 minutes, until the custard is set. Remove from the water bath and cool on wire racks for an hour. Cover and refrigerate 4 hours or overnight.
5. Preheat your broiler. Sprinkle 1 tablespoon of sugar on the top of each chilled ramekin. Return the ramekins to the baking pan and fill the pan halfway with cold water and ice cubes. Slide the pan under the broiler for a minute or less, until the sugar bubbles and turns brown. Remove from the pan.

Makes 4 individual bittersweet custards.

French Truffles

Don't let the simplicity of this recipe fool you. These hand-molded bites of pure chocolate and rich cream, teased with a hint of aged cognac, are the quintessential chocolate indulgence!

8	ounces semisweet chocolate, chopped into small pieces	2	tablespoons French cognac
⅓	cup heavy cream, warmed to room temperature	½	cup Dutch-processed cocoa powder (alkalized)

1. Place the chopped chocolate in a mixing bowl; set aside.
2. Bring the cream to a simmer, three times, removing from heat for a few seconds between simmers. Pour over the chocolate and allow to stand for one minute. Stir until smooth. Add the cognac and mix thoroughly. Cover and refrigerate.
3. When fairly solid, scoop out teaspoonfuls and roll into balls. Delicately roll in cocoa powder and place in petit four-sized cups.

Makes about 20 traditional French truffles.

Biscotti Parfait

Crunchy and smooth, sweet and tangy; this whimsical parfait filled with sophisticated treats is for your adventurous Chocolate Days!

2	ounces chèvre (goat milk cheese), softened	½	cup heavy cream, whipped
4	ounces cream cheese, softened	2	chocolate biscotti cookies, crumbled
2	tablespoons Dutch-processed (alkalized) cocoa powder, sifted	½	cup mandarin orange slices, drained
3	tablespoons powdered sugar, sifted		

1. Cream together the cheeses, cocoa powder, and sugar, with a mixer on high, until fluffy. Add two tablespoons of the whipped cream and mix.
2. By hand, using a rubber spatula, fold in the remaining whipped cream.
3. Spoon a small amount into your favorite parfait glass, layer with ⅓ of the crumbled biscotti, half of the remaining cream mixture, and ¼ cup mandarin orange slices. Repeat and top with crumbled biscotti.

Makes one rich parfait.

Bavarian Torte

Toasted hazelnuts and espresso mingle with bittersweet chocolate to bring you this European-style cake!

The Torte

8	ounces bittersweet chocolate, chopped into small pieces
1¼	cups toasted, ground hazelnuts
¾	cup unsalted butter, softened
⅔	cup sugar
5	eggs, separated and warmed to room temperature
2	tablespoons coffee liqueur
2	tablespoons instant espresso powder

Bittersweet Ganache

6	ounces bittersweet chocolate, chopped into small pieces
¼	cup unsalted butter, softened
¼	cup heavy cream
1	ounce milk chocolate, chopped into small pieces
12	mocha beans*

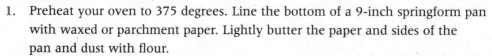

1. Preheat your oven to 375 degrees. Line the bottom of a 9-inch springform pan with waxed or parchment paper. Lightly butter the paper and sides of the pan and dust with flour.

2. *To make the torte:* Melt the chocolate in the top of a double boiler, over hot (not boiling) water, stirring until smooth; remove from heat and cool to tepid.

3. Toast and grind the hazelnuts (see "Tips," page -xiv); set aside.

4. Cream together the butter and sugar, with a mixer on high, until fluffy. Adjust mixer to medium and add the egg yolks, one at a time, beating well after each addition. Adjust your mixer to low and slowly pour in the melted chocolate, liqueur, espresso powder, and ground nuts.

5. In a clean, dry bowl beat the egg whites, with a mixer on high, until stiff peaks form. By hand, with a rubber spatula, gently fold the egg whites into the batter, in four increments.

6. Gently, pour the batter into the prepared pan and bake for about 45–50 minutes. Cool on a wire rack.

7. *To make the ganache:* Place the bittersweet chocolate and butter in a bowl; set aside. Bring the cream to a simmer, three times, removing from heat for a few seconds between each simmer, then pour over the chocolate mixture. Stir gently until smooth; avoid creating bubbles. Cool to about 90 degrees and glaze the room temperature torte. Microwave the milk chocolate, on a MEDIUM setting, for 10 seconds; remove and stir. Repeat until melted. Place in a pastry bag fitted with a writing tip and "lace" the torte. Decorate with the mocha beans.

Makes 10–12 dense servings.

*Hard cream candies shaped like coffee beans; available at most candy stores and some coffee roasting shops.

Truffle Tea Cookies

These delicate little bite-sized cookies, rolled in cocoa powder, look like French truffles and are almost as rich!

½   cup almonds
2   ounces semisweet chocolate, chopped into small pieces
¾   cup flour
3   tablespoons non-alkalized cocoa powder, sifted
6   tablespoons unsalted butter, softened

¼   cup powdered sugar, sifted
1   teaspoon chocolate liqueur
2   tablespoons finely chopped dried apricots
¼   cup Dutch-processed cocoa powder (alkalized)

1. Preheat your oven to 350 degrees. Lightly butter cookie sheets and dust with flour.
2. Toast and chop the almonds (see "Tips," page xiv); set aside.
3. Microwave the chopped chocolate, on a MEDIUM setting, for 15 seconds. Stir thoroughly. Continue, in 15 second increments, until melted; set aside and cool to tepid.
4. Sift together the flour and non-alkalized cocoa powder; set aside.
5. Cream together the butter and sugar, with a mixer on high, until fluffy. Add the liqueur and mix thoroughly. Adjust your mixer to low and gradually mix in the melted chocolate, flour mixture, nuts, and apricots, just until blended.
6. Roll into bite-size balls and bake for 12–15 minutes. Roll balls in the Dutch-processed (alkalized) cocoa while still warm. Let cool on wire racks and roll in cocoa again.

Makes about 20 tea cookies.

Chocolate Truffle Cake

For years, when I was having a Chocolate Day, I'd go to Gayle's, a world-class bakery in the seaside town of Capitola, to get a slice of the richest chocolate "cake" I'd ever tasted. The name was perfect, for the taste and texture were closer to a truffle than a cake. It broke my heart when they stopped making it; so I began a quest to duplicate it.

1   pound of Callebaut semisweet chocolate, chopped

10   tablespoons unsalted butter, softened

4   eggs, separated and warmed to room temperature

2   tablespoons chocolate liqueur

1   tablespoon flour

3   cups heavy cream

2   tablespoons powdered sugar

2   cups (about 6 ounces) dark chocolate curls (see "Tips," page xiv)

1. Preheat your oven to 425 degrees. Line the bottom of an 8-inch springform pan with waxed or parchment paper. Lightly butter the paper and sides of the pan and dust with flour.
2. Melt the chopped chocolate and butter in the top of a double boiler, over hot (not boiling) water, stirring until smooth; remove from heat and cool to tepid.
3. Beat the egg yolks, with a mixer on medium, until thick. Whisk the yolks, liqueur, and flour into the chocolate mixture.
4. In a clean, dry bowl, beat the egg whites, with a mixer on high, until stiff peaks form. By hand, using a rubber spatula, gently fold the egg whites into the chocolate mixture in four increments, taking care not to deflate the egg whites.
5. Pour into the prepared pan and bake for 15 minutes. Cool on a wire rack and refrigerate.
6. Whip the cream, using a mixer on high. When soft peaks form, sprinkle in the sugar, while continuing to beat, until stiff peaks form. Frost the cake, leveling the fallen center with the whipped cream, and cover with the chocolate curls.

Makes 12 truffle-rich slices.

Mocha Nirvana

Are you ready for the richest, most achingly delicious cookies you've ever tasted? Fasten your seat belt; one bite and we guarantee, you'll soar into nirvana!

4	ounces bittersweet chocolate, chopped	¼	teaspoon baking powder
			Pinch of salt
2	tablespoons unsalted butter, softened	1	egg, warmed to room temperature
		⅓	cup sugar
2	tablespoons flour	1	tablespoon Kahlúa liqueur
1	tablespoon cocoa powder	½	cup (3 ounces) semisweet chocolate chips
1	tablespoon instant espresso powder	¼	cup mocha beans*

*Hard cream candies shaped like coffee beans; available at most candy stores and some coffee roasting shops.

1. Preheat oven to 350 degrees and cover cookie sheets with parchment paper.
2. Melt the chocolate and butter in the top of a double boiler over hot (not boiling) water; remove from heat and cool to tepid.
3. Sift together the flour, cocoa, espresso, baking powder, and salt; set aside.
4. Beat the egg, sugar, and Kahlúa, with a mixer on high, until fluffy. Adjust your mixer to low and gradually add the melted chocolate mixture.
5. By hand, with a rubber spatula, fold the flour mixture into the chocolate mixture. *Don't overmix!* Fold in the chocolate chips and mocha beans.
6. Drop by teaspoonfuls onto the prepared sheets and bake for 10 minutes. Let them cool completely on the cookie sheets (on wire racks).

Makes about 15 cookies.

Cinnamon Swirl Bread Pudding

Here's a spicy, elegant version of a down-home favorite. And if you prefer your cinnamon toast with raisins, even better!

8	ounces semisweet chocolate, chopped into small pieces	3	slices cinnamon swirl bread
¾	cup milk	1	egg yolk, warmed to room temperature
¾	cup heavy cream	1	egg, warmed to room temperature
1	tablespoon sugar		

1. Preheat your oven to 350 degrees. Lightly butter a 4-cup souffle dish.
2. Melt the chocolate in the top of a double boiler, over hot (not boiling) water; remove from heat.
3. In a heavy-bottomed saucepan, scald the milk, cream, and sugar; remove from heat and pour into the melted chocolate; stir until smooth and cool to tepid.
4. Lightly toast the bread and cut into bite-size squares; set aside.
5. In a small bowl, whisk the egg yolk and egg. Gradually whisk the eggs into the cooled chocolate mixture.
6. Layer the chocolate mixture and toast in the souffle dish. Set aside for 15 minutes, and then bake for 45–50 minutes. Cool slightly before serving.

Makes 4 creamy servings.

Chocolate Nights

Mmmmmmm . . . and then there are Chocolate Nights. Since the days of kings and pharaohs, this "food of the gods" has been a coveted aphrodisiac and catalyst for romance. No taste or texture is quite as sensuous, especially by candlelight. So set your stage carefully, and these sinful selections will provide a slide into the kind of evenings from which legends are born.

Amourette Cacao

To celebrate your love affair with chocolate, try this petite Florentine tower. Almonds, honey, and creamy Greek cheese magically transform as they climb their stairway to chocolate heaven!

Florentines

¼ cup unsalted butter, softened
¼ cup heavy cream, warmed to room temperature
¼ cup firmly packed light brown sugar
2 tablespoons honey
2 tablespoons light corn syrup
⅓ cup flour
1½ cups sliced almonds

Ganache Base

4 ounces semisweet chocolate, chopped into small pieces
2 tablespoons heavy cream, warmed to room temperature
1 tablespoon Greek manouri cheese, softened
½ teaspoon honey
1 tablespoon amaretto liqueur

Center Layer

3 ounces semisweet chocolate, chopped into small pieces
¼ cup heavy cream, warmed to room temperature
¼ cup Greek manouri cheese, softened
1 teaspoon honey
1 tablespoon chocolate liqueur
¼ teaspoon ground ginger

Whipped Crown

2 ounces semisweet chocolate, chopped into small pieces
1 tablespoon Greek manouri cheese, softened
½ teaspoon honey
½ cup heavy cream, chilled
2 tablespoons *each*, chocolate and amaretto liqueur
2 tablespoons dark chocolate curls

1. *To make the Florentines:* Preheat your oven to 350 degrees. Use nonstick cookie sheets or lightly butter and flour aluminum sheets.

2. In a heavy-bottomed saucepan, brown the butter over medium heat. Remove the pan from the heat and stir in the cream, sugar, honey, and corn syrup. Return the pan to the heat and bring the mixture to a boil, stirring constantly. Again, remove the pan from the heat, sprinkle in the flour, and mix thoroughly. Add the almonds and blend well.

3. Drop teaspoonfuls of the mixture onto the prepared cookie sheets and spread into even circles with the back of the teaspoon. Bake for 8–12 minutes, until the edges are golden brown and the centers are bubbling. Cool on wire racks.

4. *To make the ganache base:* Place the chocolate in a bowl. In a small saucepan, whisk together the cream, cheese, and honey, and bring to a simmer. Pour the hot cream mixture over the chocolate, allow to stand for one minute. Gently stir until the chocolate is completely melted. Add the liqueur, mix thoroughly, cover, and refrigerate to the consistency of frosting.

5. *To make the center layer:* Place the chopped chocolate in a bowl. In a small saucepan, bring the cream to a simmer. Pour the hot cream over the chocolate and allow to stand for one minute. Gently stir until the chocolate is completely melted; cool to tepid. With a mixer on high, beat the cheese until fluffy. Adjust your mixer to low and slowly add the chocolate mixture, honey, liqueur, and ginger. Beat just until mixed; cover and refrigerate to the consistency of softened cream cheese.

6. *To make the whipped crown:* Melt the chocolate, cheese, and honey, in the top of a double boiler, over hot (not boiling) water, stirring until smooth; remove from heat and cool to tepid. In a chilled bowl, with chilled beaters, whip the cream until firm peaks form. Carefully and slowly pour the tepid chocolate mixture into the whipped cream until just barely blended. *Don't overmix* or the mixture will become sandy in texture. Cover and refrigerate.

7. *To assemble the towers:* Decorate two dessert plates with 1 tablespoon *each* of chocolate and amaretto liqueur. Place one Florentine in the center of each plate. Place the ganache in a pastry bag fitted with a medium star tip and pipe a layer on each Florentine. Top each with a Florentine. Place the center mixture in a pastry bag fitted with a medium star tip and pipe a layer on each Florentine. Top each with another Florentine. Place the whipped topping in a pastry bag fitted with a medium star tip and crown each Florentine. Top with chocolate curls.

Makes two glorious towers!

Tuxedo Strawberries

These are show-stoppers! Giant, luscious, long-stemmed strawberries all dressed up in chocolate tuxedos!

6   giant, long-stemmed strawberries

3   ounces white chocolate, tempered
(see "Tips," page xiii)

4   ounces dark chocolate, tempered
(see "Tips," page xiii)

1. Cover a cookie sheet with waxed paper.
2. Wash the strawberries and *dry them thoroughly* with paper towels. Place the strawberries on the cookie sheet and notice how they lie.

3. Pick the berries up by their stems (one at a time), holding up the green top as well, and dip their front halves (the side that faced up when lying on the cookie sheet) in the white tempered chocolate. Put them back on the cookie sheet, chocolate side up, to cool. You've just put their shirts on!

4. When cool, pick them up, again by the stem holding the green tops up, and dip each side at an angle, in the tempered dark chocolate, so that a "V" is formed on the front of each berry. Now they're in their jackets!

5. To help them with their bow ties and buttons, put the remaining dark chocolate in a pastry bag fitted with a writing tip. Draw a horizontally elongated "x" at the top and center of the white "V." Color in the sides of the "x." Lightly touch the berry three times down the middle of the "V" to form the buttons.

6. Enjoy immediately or store in a cool, dry place for up to 24 hours. (Refrigerating will cause the chocolate to "sweat.")

Makes 6, in formal attire!

Pâte Grand Marnier

This velvety loaf of rich chocolate, cloaked in toasted hazelnuts and crowned with bits of candied orange peel, is achingly delicious alone or spread on light wafers!

12	ounces semisweet chocolate, chopped into small pieces	1	tablespoon superfine sugar
¼	cup unsalted butter, softened	4	tablespoons Grand Marnier liqueur
½	cup heavy cream	1½	cups hazelnuts
2	egg yolks, warmed to room temperature	⅓	cup finely chopped candied orange peel
2	eggs, warmed to room temperature		Light wafers, Florentines, or pieces of angel cake

1. Lightly oil a loaf pan and line with plastic wrap, leaving an overhang on all sides.
2. Melt the chocolate and butter, in the top of a double boiler over hot (not boiling) water, stirring until smooth; remove from heat and cool to tepid.
3. Whip the cream, with a mixer on high, until soft peaks form; refrigerate.
4. Whisk the egg yolks, eggs, sugar, and liqueur in the top of a double boiler, which is touching the hot (not boiling) water on its bottom, until the sugar dissolves and the mixture reaches 160 degrees. Remove from heat and beat, with a mixer on medium, until the mixture becomes thick and pale; cool to tepid.
5. By hand, using a rubber spatula, gently fold 1/2 the whipped cream into the chocolate mixture. Slowly fold the chocolate mixture into the egg mixture. Gently fold the remaining whipped cream into the chocolate mixture and scrape into the prepared pan; refrigerate.
6. Toast, skin, and chop the hazelnuts (see "Tips," page xiv).
7. When firm, carefully unmold onto your favorite dessert plate. Cover the sides with the chopped nuts, the top with candied orange peel, and surround the pâte with wafers!

Makes 12 to 16 servings.

Coupe Glacée Café

I found the inspiration for this elegant, upside-down, frosty "cup of coffee" at a terraced cafe overlooking the Côte d'Azur, on a warm, balmy Chocolate Night!

Chocolate Whipped Cream

½   cup heavy cream

1   tablespoon superfine sugar

1   teaspoon Dutch-processed (alkalized) cocoa powder

Espresso Fudge Sauce

½   cup heavy cream, warmed to room temperature

2   tablespoons dark brown sugar

1   teaspoon instant espresso powder

3   ounces bittersweet chocolate, chopped into small pieces

1   tablespoon unsalted butter, softened

5   tablespoons coffee liqueur

2   scoops of coffee gelato

2   mocha beans*

1. *To make the chocolate whipped cream:* Beat the cream with a mixer on high, until soft peaks form. Sprinkle in the sugar and cocoa powder and continue beating until stiff peaks form; refrigerate.

2. *To make the espresso fudge sauce:* Place the cream in a heavy-bottomed saucepan and simmer for 15 minutes. Stir in the brown sugar and espresso powder. When the sugar is dissolved, remove from the heat and stir in the bittersweet chocolate, butter, and 1 tablespoon of the coffee liqueur; stir until smooth and refrigerate.

3. *To assemble:* Place 2 tablespoons of the remaining coffee liqueur in each of two small goblets. Use a spoon or place the chocolate whipped cream in a pastry bag fitted with a star tip, and pipe a "pillow" in each goblet, reserving 2 tablespoons of the whipped cream. In the center of each "pillow," gently place a scoop of gelato. Top with the espresso fudge sauce, the remaining 2 tablespoons whipped cream, and mocha beans.

Makes two coupes.

*Hard cream candies, shaped like coffee beans; available at most candy stores and some coffee roasting shops.

Crème Praline

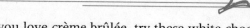

If you love crème brûlée, try these white chocolate custard cups crowned with sweet praline and buttery pecans. They'll capture your heart!

1½	cups heavy cream	2	tablespoons toasted, chopped pecans
¼	cup superfine sugar		
6	ounces white chocolate, chopped into small pieces	4	teaspoons *each*, praline and chocolate liqueur
1	teaspoon vanilla	2	tablespoons crumbled praline or honeycomb candy
4	egg yolks		

1. Preheat your oven to 350 degrees. Place 4 ramekins in a baking pan.
2. Heat the cream and sugar, in the top of a double boiler over hot (not boiling) water, stirring until the sugar is dissolved. Add the chocolate, stirring until melted; remove from heat and cool to tepid.
3. Whisk the vanilla and egg yolks together. Slowly, add the cream mixture and continue whisking until thoroughly mixed.
4. Spoon into the ramekins and pour hot water into the baking pan so that the water comes halfway up the sides of the ramekins. Bake for 45–50 minutes, until the custard is set. Remove from the water bath and cool on wire racks for an hour. Cover and refrigerate.
5. Just before serving: Top each ramekin with the pecans, 1 teaspoon *each* of the praline and chocolate liqueurs, and the crumbled candy!

Makes 4 sweet crèmes.

Fondue Chambord

Nothing is quite as romantic as sharing this warm, rich pot of raspberry-laced dark chocolate!

⅓ cup heavy cream
2 tablespoons light corn syrup
6 ounces semisweet chocolate, chopped into small pieces

2 tablespoons Chambord liqueur
Bite-sized pieces of angel cake, pound cake, or fresh fruit

1. In a heavy-bottomed saucepan, bring the cream and the corn syrup to a gentle boil.
2. Remove from heat and add the chocolate, stirring until smooth. Add the liqueur and blend thoroughly.
3. Transfer to a warmer or fondue pot and dip the bits of cake and fresh fruit.

Makes more than enough for the two of you!

Eggnog Bombe

A simple genoise, soaked with Cointreau; ice cream, laced with white chocolate and brandy; and a crown of spiced whipped cream . . . here's an elegant way to snuggle in with eggnog, year-round!

Genoise (sponge cake)

6	tablespoons unsalted butter
1	teaspoon vanilla
1	cup cake flour
1	teaspoon baking powder
¼	cup cocoa powder
4	eggs, warmed to room temperature
2	egg yolks, warmed to room temperature
½	cup superfine sugar
2	tablespoons Cointreau liqueur

White Chocolate Chunk Ice Cream

2	cups French vanilla ice cream, softened
4	ounces white chocolate, chopped into small chunks
2	tablespoons brandy

Spiced Whipped Cream

2	cups heavy cream, chilled
½	cup powdered sugar
1	teaspoon powdered allspice

1. Preheat your oven to 350 degrees. Line the bottom of an 11 × 17-inch baking pan with waxed or parchment paper. Lightly butter the paper and sides of the pan and dust with flour. Lightly oil one 2 cup, or two 1 cup, domed bowl(s). Line the bowl(s) with plastic wrap, leaving an overhang all the way around.

2. *To make the genoise:* In a heavy-bottomed saucepan, melt the butter slowly with-out stirring. Skim the foam off and remove the clear oil center. Combine this clear oil with the vanilla and keep lukewarm.

3. Sift together the flour, baking powder, and cocoa powder; set aside.

4. In the top of a double boiler, over hot (not boiling) water, whisk the eggs and egg yolks with the sugar. When the eggs are lukewarm, transfer to a mixing bowl and, with a mixer on high, beat until thick.

5. By hand, using a rubber spatula, gently but quickly fold in the flour mixture in 3 increments, until just blended. Gently fold in the butter mixture in 4 increments. Spread evenly in the prepared pan and bake for 12–15 minutes, until the top springs back when lightly touched. Cool on wire racks. When cool, cut a circle (or circles) the size of the inside rim of your domed bowl(s).

6. *To make the white chocolate chunk ice cream:* With a mixer on low, cream together the ice cream, chocolate, and brandy. Fill the prepared domed bowl(s) ¾ full, cover, and freeze.

7. *To make the spiced whipped cream:* Whip the chilled cream, with a mixer on high. When soft peaks form, sprinkle in the powdered sugar and allspice. Whip until stiff peaks form and refrigerate.

8. *To assemble, just before serving:* Place the genoise circle(s) on your favorite dessert plate(s) and sprinkle with Cointreau. Unmold the ice cream and place on top of the genoise to form a dome. Fill a pastry bag, fitted with a medium star tip, with the spiced whipped cream and cover the entire bombe(s).

Makes one bombe for two, or two individual bombes.

Tiramisu Chocolat

Sweet Italian cream cheese, layered between rum and Kahlúa-soaked ladyfingers, topped with grated chocolate; it's no wonder this little pastry has stolen hearts all over the world. There's only one way to improve on this romantic treat . . . more *chocolat!*

Chocolate Ladyfingers

¾	cup cake flour
¼	cup cocoa powder
1	teaspoon baking powder
¼	teaspoon salt
2	eggs, warmed to room temperature
½	cup superfine sugar
1	tablespoon chocolate liqueur

Soaking Liqueur

½	teaspoon espresso powder
1	tablespoon coffee liqueur
1	tablespoon rum
¼	cup brewed coffee, hot

Creamy Filling

4	ounces mascarpone, softened
1	egg yolk, warmed to room temperature
1	tablespoon superfine sugar
1	tablespoon coffee liqueur
1	tablespoon rum
½	cup (about 3 ounces) milk chocolate shavings (see "Tips," page xiv)
4	tablespoons (about 1 ounce) milk chocolate curls (see "Tips," page xiv)

1. *To make the chocolate ladyfingers:* Preheat oven to 375 degrees. Cover cookie sheets with parchment paper.
2. Sift together the flour, cocoa powder, baking powder, and salt; set aside.
3. Beat together the eggs, sugar, and liqueur, with a mixer on medium, until fluffy.
4. Sift in a small amount of the flour mixture and gently fold by hand using a rubber spatula. Continue until all the flour is incorporated and the texture is smooth.
5. Fill a pastry bag, fitted with a medium plain tip, and pipe 3-inch fingers onto your prepared cookie sheets. Bake for 10–12 minutes; cool on wire racks.
6. *To make the soaking liqueur:* Stir the espresso powder, liqueur, and rum into the hot coffee; set aside to cool.
7. *To make the creamy filling:* Whip the cheese, with a mixer on high, until fluffy. In the top of a double boiler over simmering water, whisk together the egg yolk and sugar, until the sugar is dissolved and the mixture is hot to the touch. Remove from the heat, stir in the liqueur and rum, and cool to tepid. Whisk the egg mixture into the cheese. Gently fold in the chocolate shavings, creating a "speckled" effect.
8. *To assemble:* Place a square of lady fingers on each of two dessert plates. Sprinkle with half the soaking liqueur. Layer with half the creamy filling. Top with another square of ladyfingers, the remaining soaking liqueur, and the rest of the filling. Top with the chocolate curls.

Makes two tiramisus.

Fire & Ice . . . Finger Paints D'Amour!

By the soft glow of candlelight, with music that brings out your relaxed, creative side, this ultimate chocolate indulgence engages all your senses!

16	ounces semisweet chocolate, chopped	1½	cups heavy cream
2	tablespoons light corn syrup	2	tablespoons cinnamon schnapps
¼	cup unsalted butter	2	tablespoons peppermint schnapps

1. Melt the chocolate, corn syrup, and butter in the top of a double boiler over hot (not boiling) water, stirring until smooth.
2. In a small saucepan, bring the cream to a simmer, three times, removing from heat for a few seconds between simmers. Pour the hot cream into the chocolate mixture and stir until smooth.
3. Divide the chocolate mixture between two heatproof bowls. In one bowl add the cinnamon schnapps and mix thoroughly. In the other bowl add the peppermint schnapps and mix thoroughly. Cool to 99 degrees, transfer to finger bowls, and choose your canvas!

Makes enough for two paintings!

Resources

When we started making our own truffles and chocolate specialities, we had a difficult time finding chocolate thermometers (different from candy thermometers), spiral dipping forks, coverture in "ribbons" and "calets" (chocolate which is "pre-chopped" for faster and easier melting), and other chocolate necessities. So we set up what's grown into "all things CHOCOLATE," a mail-order source for home chocolatiers.

Here's how you can get our catalog and those of other fine chocolate and pastryware suppliers:

all things CHOCOLATE
P.O. Box 561
Los Gatos, CA 95031
Domestic and imported coverture and coating chocolates, mocha beans, supplies, and tools, for the home chocolatier. Mail-order catalog.

Casa de Fruta
6680 Pacheco Pass Highway
Hollister, CA 95023
(800) 543-1702
Gourmet nuts and dried fruits. Mail-order catalog and retail stores.

J. B. Prince Company
29 West 38th Street
New York, NY 10018
Books and tools for the foodservice professional. Mail-order catalog.

La Cuisine–The Cook's Resource

323 Cameron Street
Alexandria, VA 22314
(800) 521-1176
Classic cookware, equipment, tools, and imported chocolate.

Parrish's Cake Decorating Supplies

225 W. 146th Street
Gardena, CA 90248
(800) 736-8443
Cake and candy equipment, tools, supplies, and domestic chocolate.

Sweet Celebrations

7009 Washington Avenue South
Edina, MN 55439
(800) 328-6722
Dessert and candy making supplies, domestic and imported chocolate.

Williams-Sonoma

P.O. Box 7456
San Francisco, CA 94120
Gourmet bakeware, foods, flavorings, and imported chocolate.

Index

Almonds
  Amourette Cacao, 87
    Chocolate Apple
      Streusel, 22
    Chocolate Ecstasy, 46
    Truffle Tea Cookies, 78
Amourette Cacao, 87
Angel Berry Trifle, 34
Apples
  Chocolate Apple
    Streusel, 22
Apricot
  Truffle Tea Cookies, 78
Bananas
  Banana Bliss, 5
  Banana Fudge
    Muffins, 36
  Banana Split Trifle, 54
Biscotti Parfait, 75
Bittersweet Chocolate
  Bavarian Torte, 76
  Bittersweet Creme
    Brulee, 72
  Capp Cakes, 44
  Chunky Junkie Bundt, 28
  Coupe Glacee Cafe, 94

Mocha L'Orange
  Slush, 33
Mocha Nirvana, 82
  Starry Night Muffins, 24
Bittersweet Creme Brulee, 72
Blackberry
  Angel Berry Trifle, 34
Bombes
  Eggnog Bombe, 98
  Peanut Butter Fudge
    Bombe, 6
Bread Pudding
  Cinnamon Swirl Bread
    Pudding, 84
Brownies
  Chocolate Pizza, 58
  Double Chocolate
    Brownies, 18
  Liar's Dice, 52
  Mari's Brownie Binge, 11
Buttercream Layer Cake, 20
Cakes
  Angel Berry Trifle, 34
  Banana Bliss, 5
  Banana Split Trifle, 54
  Bavarian Torte, 76

  Buttercream Layer
    Cake, 20
  Chocolate Apple
    Streusel, 22
  Chocolate Ecstasy, 46
  Chocolate Pound
    Cake, 26
  Chocolate Truffle
    Cake, 80
  Chunky Junkie Bundt, 28
  Hot Fudge Pudding
    Cake, 16
  Irish Cream Cheese
    Cups, 40
  Lemon Cream
    Dreams, 60
  Peanut Butter Cup
    Cakes, 64
  Raspberry Crowns, 70
  Tiramisu Chocolat, 100
Candy
  Candy Bar Mousse, 7
  Chocolate Pizza, 58
  French Truffles, 74
  Peaches and Cream
    Truffles, 66

Peanut Butter Cup
    Cakes, 64
    Rainbow Crispies, 51
    Tuxedo Strawberries, 90
Candy Bar Mousse, 7
CappCakes, 44
Cashews
    Banana Fudge
        Muffins, 36
Charlottes
    Twinkies Charlotte, 9
Cheesecakes
    Irish Cream Cheese
        Cups, 40
    Tri-Chocolate Pie, 62
Cherries
    Cherries Oreo!, 3
    Cocoa Butter Cookies, 30
    CocoLocos, 42
    Lemon Cream Dreams, 60
Chocolate
    curls and shavings, xiv
    melting, xii
    microwaving, xiii
    storing, xii
    tempering, xiii
    tips, xi
    types, xv
Chocolate Apple Streusel, 22
Chocolate Ecstasy, 46

Chocolate Mint Clouds, 48
Chocolate Pizza, 58
Chocolate Pound Cake, 26
Cinnamon
    Chocolate Apple
        Streusel, 22
    Cinnamon Swirl Bread
        Pudding, 84
    Fire & Ice, Finger Paints
        D'Amour, 102
    Mocha L'Orange Slush 33
Cinnamon Swirl Bread
    Pudding, 84
Chocolate Truffle Cake, 80
Cognac
    Eggnog Bombe, 98
    French Truffles, 74
    Pate Grand Marnier, 92
Chunky Junkie Bundt, 28
Cocoa Butter Cookies, 30
Coconut
    Macadamia
        Macaroons, 56
Coffee
    Bavarian Torte, 76
    CappCakes, 44
    Coupe Glacee Cafe, 94
    Icedwiches, 38
    Mocha L'Orange
        Slush, 33

Mocha Nirvana, 82
Quick Cafe Mocha, 4
Tiramisu Chocolat, 100
Cookies
    Biscotti Parfait, 75
    Cherries Oreo!, 3
    Chocolate Mint
        Clouds, 48
    Cocoa Butter Cookies, 30
    CocoLocos, 42
    Macadamia
        Macaroons, 56
    Mocha Nirvana, 82
    Peanut Butter
        Fudge Bombe, 6
    Rainbow Crispies, 51
    Strawberry S'mores, 8
    Toll House Chunks, 14
    Truffle Tea Cookies, 78
Creme/Custard
    Bittersweet Creme
        Brulee, 72
    Creme Praline, 96
Creme Praline, 96
Double Chocolate
    Brownies, 18
Drinks
    Mocha L'Orange
        Slush, 33
    Mystic Mint Chiller, 10

Quick Cafe Mocha, 4
Fire & Ice, Finger Paints
    D'Amour, 102
Fondue Chambord, 97
French Truffles, 74
Frosting
    bittersweet ganache, 76
    chocolate buttercream, 20
    chocolate whipped cream,
        11, 94
    espresso fudge sauce, 94
    Irish Cream, 52
    lemon buttercream, 60
    marshmellow, 51
    peanut buttercream, 64
    spiced whipped cream, 98
    whipped cream, 80
    white chocolate, 52
Frozen Yogurt
    Angel Berry Trifle, 34
Fruit
    Angel Berry Trifle, 34
    Banana Bliss, 5
    Banana Fudge
        Muffins, 36
    Banana Split Trifle, 54
    Biscotti Parfait, 75
    Cherries Oreo!, 3
    Chocolate Apple
        Streusel, 22

Chocolate Pizza, 58
Cocoa Butter Cookies, 30
CocoLocos, 42
Lemon Cream Dreams, 60
Macadamia
    Macaroons, 56
Peaches and Cream
    Truffles, 66
Strawberry S'mores, 8
Truffle Tea Cookies, 78
Tuxedo Strawberries, 90
Fudge
    Banana Fudge
        Muffins, 36
    espresso fudge sauce, 94
    Hot Fudge Pudding
        Cake, 16
    Mari's Brownie Binge, 11
    Peanut Butter Fudge
        Bombe, 6
    Starry Night Muffins, 24
Gelato
    Coupe Glacee Cafe, 94
Ginger
    Amourette Cacao, 87
Hazelnuts
    Bavarian Torte, 76
    Pate Grand Marnier, 92
Hot Fudge Pudding
    Cake, 16

Ice Cream
    Coupe Glacee Cafe, 94
    Eggnog Bombe, 98
    Mari's Brownie Binge, 11
    Mystic Mint Chiller, 10
    Peanut Butter Fudge
        Bombe, 6
    Quick Cafe Mocha, 4
    Twinkies Charlotte, 9
Iced Milk
    Icedwiches, 38
    Mocha L'Orange
        Slush, 33
Icedwiches, 38
Irish Cream
    Irish Cream Cheese
        Cups, 40
    Liar's Dice, 52
    Peaches and Cream
        Truffles, 66
Lemon Cream Dreams, 60
Liar's Dice, 52
Macadamia Macroons, 56
Mari's Brownie Binge, 11
Marshmellow
    Banana Split Trifle, 54
    Rainbow Crispies, 51
Meringue
    Chocolate Mint
        Clouds, 48

Icedwiches, 38
Milk Chocolate
    Banana Split Trifle, 54
    Candy Bar Mousse, 7
    Chocolate Pizza, 58
    Cocoa Butter
        Cookies, 30
    Double Chocolate
        Brownies, 18
    Macadamia
        Macaroons, 56
    Peanut Butter Cup
        Cakes, 64
    Tiramisu Chocolat, 100
    Toll House Chunks, 14
    Tri-Chocolate Pie, 62
Mint
    Chocolate Mint
        Clouds, 48
    Fire & Ice, Finger Paints
        D'Amour, 102
    Mystic Mint Chiller, 10
Mocha
    Bavarian Torte, 76
    CappCakes, 44
    Coupe Glacee Cafe, 94
    Icedwiches, 38
    Mocha L'Orange
        Slush, 33
    Mocha Nirvana, 82

Quick Cafe Mocha, 4
Tiramisu Chocolat, 100
Mocha L'Orange Slush, 33
Mocha Nirvana, 82
Mousse
    Candy Bar Mousse, 7
Muffins
    Banana Fudge
        Muffins, 36
    Starry Night Muffins, 24
Mystic Mint Chiller, 10
Nuts
    Amourette Cacao, 87
    Banana Fudge
        Muffins, 36
    Banana Split Trifle, 54
    Bavarian Torte, 76
    Chocolate Ecstasy, 46
    Chocolate Pizza, 58
    Double Chocolate
        Brownies, 18
    grinding, xiv
    Macadamia
        Macaroons, 56
    Pate Grand Marnier, 92
    Peanut Butter Cup
        Cakes, 64
    Peanut Butter Fudge
        Bombe, 6
    toasting, xiv

Toll House Chunks, 14
Truffle Tea Cookies, 78
Twinkies Charlotte, 9
Orange
    Biscotti Parfait, 75
    Eggnog Bombe, 98
    Pate Grand Marnier, 92
    Mocha L'Orange
        Slush, 33
Parfaits
    Biscotti Parfait, 75
    Coupe Glacee Cafe, 94
Pate Grand Marnier, 92
Peaches and Cream
        Truffles, 66
Peanuts
    Banana Split Trifle, 54
    Peanut Butter Cup
        Cakes, 64
    Peanut Butter Fudge
        Bombe, 6
Pecans
    Toll House Chunks, 14
    Twinkies Charlotte, 9
Pies
    Tri-Chocolate Pie, 62
Pound Cake
    Banana Bliss, 5
    Chocolate Pound
        Cake, 26

Praline
  Creme Praline, 96
  Twinkies Charlotte, 9
Pudding
  Banana Bliss, 5
  Cinnamon Swirl Bread
    Pudding, 84
  Hot Fudge Pudding
    Cake, 16
Quick Cafe Mocha, 4
Rainbow Crispies, 51
Raspberry
  Angel Berry Trifle, 34
  Fondue Chambord, 97
  Icedwiches, 38
  Raspberry Crowns, 70
Raspberry Crowns, 70
Semisweet Chocolate
  Amourette Cacao, 87
  Banana Fudge Muffins, 36
  Buttercream Layer
    Cake, 20
  Capp Cakes, 44
  Chocolate Apple
    Streusel, 22
  Chocolate Ecstasy, 46
  Chocolate Pound
    Cake, 26
  Chocolate Truffle Cake, 80
  Chunky Junkie Bundt, 28

Cinnamon Swirl Bread
  Pudding, 84
Double Chocolate
  Brownies, 18
Fire & Ice, Finger Paints
  D'Amour, 102
Fondue Chambord, 97
French Truffles, 74
Hot Fudge Pudding
  Cake, 16
Pate Grand Marnier, 92
Raspberry Crowns, 70
Tuxedo Strawberries, 90
Sorbet
  Angel Berry Trifle, 34
Strawberry
  Angel Berry Trifle, 34
  Banana Split Trifle, 54
  Chocolate Pizza, 58
  Fondue Chambord, 97
  Strawberry S'Mores, 8
  Tuxedo Strawberries, 90
Tiramisu Chocolat, 100
Toll House Chunks, 14
Tortes
  Bavarian Torte, 76
  Chocolate Ecstasy, 46
  Chocolate Truffle
    Cake, 80
  Raspberry Crowns, 70

Trifle
  Angel Berry Trifle, 34
  Banana Split Trifle, 54
Truffle Tea Cookies, 78
Truffles
  French Truffles, 74
  Peaches and Cream
    Truffles, 66
Twinkies Charlotte, 9
Walnuts
  Double Chocolate
    Brownies, 18
White Chocolate
  Cherries Oreo!, 3
  Creme Praline, 96
  Eggnog Bombe, 98
  Irish Cream Cheese
    Cups, 40
  Lemon Cream Dreams, 60
  Liar's Dice, 52
  Macadamia
    Macaroons, 56
  Peaches and Cream
    Truffles, 66
  Starry Night Muffins, 24
  Tri-Chocolate Pie, 62
  Tuxedo Strawberries, 90

INTERNATIONAL CONVERSION CHART

These are not exact equivalents: they've been slightly rounded to make measuring easier.

LIQUID MEASUREMENTS

American	Imperial	Metric	Australian
2 tablespoons (1 oz.)	1 fl. oz.	30 ml	1 tablespoon
¼ cup (2 oz.)	2 fl. oz.	60 ml	2 tablespoons
⅓ cup (3 oz.)	3 fl. oz.	80 ml	¼ cup
½ cup (4 oz.)	4 fl. oz.	125 ml	⅓ cup
⅔ cup (5 oz.)	5 fl. oz.	165 ml	½ cup
¾ cup (6 oz.)	6 fl. oz.	185 ml	⅔ cup
1 cup (8 oz.)	8 fl. oz.	250 ml	¾ cup

SPOON MEASUREMENTS

American	Metric
¼ teaspoon	1 ml
½ teaspoon	2 ml
1 teaspoon	5 ml
1 tablepoon	15 ml

WEIGHTS

US/UK	Metric
1 oz.	30 grams (g)
2 oz.	60 g
4 oz. (¼ lb)	125 g
5 oz. (⅓ lb)	155 g
6 oz.	185 g
7 oz.	220 g
8 oz. (½ lb)	250 g
10 oz.	315 g
12 oz. (¾ lb)	375 g
14 oz.	440 g
16 oz. (1 lb)	500 g
2 lbs.	1 kg

OVEN TEMPERATURES

Fahrenheit	Centigrade	Gas
250	120	½
300	150	2
325	160	3
350	180	4
375	190	5
400	200	6
450	230	8